The Second
Civil War

The Second Civil

WAR

*A citizen's guide to healing
our fractured nation*

PETER MONTOYA

with Darcy Hogan

Orange County, California, USA

© 2021 by Peter Montoya
with Darcy Hogan

ISBN 978-1-7372067-3-6

Illustrations by Carmen Ziervogel.
Printed in the United States of America.

TABLE

OF

CONTENTS

News, Media, and Personalities: Fear the fearmonger

Social Media: Rage against the outrage machine

Victory: Play the only winning move

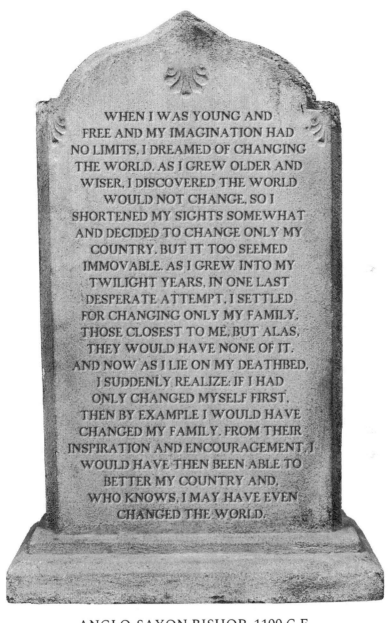

WHEN I WAS YOUNG AND
FREE AND MY IMAGINATION HAD
NO LIMITS, I DREAMED OF CHANGING
THE WORLD. AS I GREW OLDER AND
WISER, I DISCOVERED THE WORLD
WOULD NOT CHANGE, SO I
SHORTENED MY SIGHTS SOMEWHAT
AND DECIDED TO CHANGE ONLY MY
COUNTRY. BUT IT TOO SEEMED
IMMOVABLE. AS I GREW INTO MY
TWILIGHT YEARS, IN ONE LAST
DESPERATE ATTEMPT, I SETTLED
FOR CHANGING ONLY MY FAMILY,
THOSE CLOSEST TO ME, BUT ALAS,
THEY WOULD HAVE NONE OF IT.
AND NOW AS I LIE ON MY DEATHBED,
I SUDDENLY REALIZE: IF I HAD
ONLY CHANGED MYSELF FIRST,
THEN BY EXAMPLE I WOULD HAVE
CHANGED MY FAMILY. FROM THEIR
INSPIRATION AND ENCOURAGEMENT, I
WOULD HAVE THEN BEEN ABLE TO
BETTER MY COUNTRY AND,
WHO KNOWS, I MAY HAVE EVEN
CHANGED THE WORLD.

ANGLO-SAXON BISHOP, 1100 C.E.
*Engraved on his tombstone
in the crypts of Westminster Abbey.*

I PLEDGE
ALLEGIANCE

"It is high time that we stopped thinking
politically as Republicans and Democrats
about elections and started thinking
patriotically as Americans...."

MARGARET CHASE SMITH
Former Member of the U.S. Senate and House of Representatives

O n seeing the title of this book, no doubt you began to wonder—who wrote this? What is their angle? Which party will they peg as the "villain" in this war? *What is this author's political affiliation?* You are either going to be disappointed or pleasantly surprised when I tell you *I do not have one.* I have been party-free since the early 2000s and have voted on both sides of the aisle.

My name is Peter Montoya, and I am an *American*. In terms of my political allegiance, that is it and that is all. My goal is unity—to help my fellow compatriots better empathize, understand, and cooperate with one another to heal our country's great divide and solve our nation's problems. The only way to do that effectively, by my estimation, is to approach these issues without party bias, blame, or shame, and that is precisely what I hope you will find in the pages that follow.

As I am wrapping up the final edit and preparing to place this book in the publisher's hands, we are nearing the end of the first quarter of 2021. The political chasm has become deeper and more concerning than at any other point I can recall in my lifetime. I feel as though I have seen more concentrated, hateful, and riotous events in the past year than in the past few decades *combined*, and I get the sense that there is a loading magma chamber beneath a super volcano of violence building toward an explosion that will blow our country apart.

How can this be?

In the days and months following the attacks on 9/11, patriotism was at an all-time high, and our country experienced a renewed sense of unity that was truly remarkable. So much so that when then-president George W. Bush gave his famous speech on the still-smoking wreckage of the Twin Towers, even some of his most ardent opponents were moved, and they rallied behind him. Suddenly our petty in-fighting seemed profoundly insignificant. Displays of national pride went up in every city overnight. American flags sold out nationwide. For a moment, party lines dissolved and we were all, simply, Americans. In less than twenty-four hours we became *re*united.

Why?

Must we collectively experience profound loss and fear to come together as a nation? Must we have a common outside enemy to stop vilifying one another within our borders?

No. **Americans are capable of unity, despite our political differences and without the supplement of a shared adversary.** I've spent decades speaking to and training thousands of individuals, organizations, and corporations—helping them navigate everything from dealing with anxiety and being overwhelmed to how to be more cooperative and productive at work—and along the way I've studied and incorporated the science of togetherness. I've seen first hand how small changes can effect big change, and how seemingly insurmountable problems can be overcome with work and dedication. I know we can learn to hold opposing views without enmity, putting country and humanity before party affiliations.

But there is no time to waste. The events of the last several years are propelling us toward a second American civil war, the impact of which could be catastrophic not only within the United States but around the globe, even posing a threat to human civilization. We are so busy fighting each other that we are not paying attention to other existential threats building.

This book is intended not only to illuminate the danger of our current trajectory but also to illustrate how we have put ourselves in this precarious position and, most importantly, **what we as individuals can do to deescalate the conflict and work toward reunification.**

The content of this book may be uncomfortable at times. While it is intended to help bring about positive change—in your life and the lives of others—the subject matter, by its very nature, tends to be divisive. I will do my best to ensure the text remains balanced and neutral, but you will need to do your part, as well. That means keeping an open mind and realizing that, at times, the included stories will feature individuals from a party you may disagree with. This does not imply, and should not be construed to mean, that I am favoring any party over another. On the contrary, I am intentionally including examples from across the left/right spectrum specifically to ensure this book resonates with everyone, regardless of their current views or affiliations.

Anyone reading this will, at times, think that I'm implying their views are wrong. (*I'm not.*) Anyone reading this will, at times, think that I'm implying their views are right. (*Nope, I'm not.*) At some point you will feel very vulnerable, or even attacked, as you realize how you may have contributed to the growing conflict despite your good intentions. All I can say is this: please, *read on.*

My allegiance is to the success of our country and all of humanity, not

There is nothing which I dread so much as a division of the republic into two great parties, each arranged under its leader, and concerting measures in opposition to each other. This, in my humble apprehension, is to be dreaded as the greatest political evil under our Constitution.

JOHN ADAMS

to one party over another. To be partisan is to put the interests of a party—or a group of people—over the interests of your country. *Patriotism* is to incur a cost for the benefit of your compatriots, and often a cost that is inconvenient or disagreeable to you. Once you complete this book, you will understand why I do not have a party affiliation.

CHAPTER ONE

POLITICS IS THE
NEW RELIGION

"The whole aim of practical politics
is to keep the populace alarmed
(and hence clamorous to be led to safety)
by menacing it with an endless series of
hobgoblins, all of them imaginary."

H.L. MENCKEN

American Scholar, Journalist, Satirist

F or the first time in over 150 years, Americans fear other Americans more than anyone else. Our greatest enemies are our fellow citizens, and we despise one another more than at any time since the American Civil War. *And over what?* Most wars have been fought over meaningful dividing lines, such as land, resources, or individual rights. In 1861 we had clear dividing lines: Slavery, and State versus Federal powers. What are the dividing lines today? The "other side" is insane? Irrational? Unreasonable? This war is being fought partly over *status* (which group gets to say "we're better than you") and partly over *culture*—but when each "side" has a different vision for America, whose will win?

In the summer of 2018, a survey was conducted in which Americans were asked *"How likely is it that the United States will experience a second civil war sometime in the next five years?"* A staggering 42% of those surveyed felt it was either "likely" or "very likely."[1a] Let that sink in for a moment. ***More than 1 in 3 Americans feel we may soon be amid a second civil war.***

You'll notice that when I reference the "other side" I include quotation marks. If we were face-to-face you would see me making air-quotes. That is because the "other side" is a construct you have invented. It is you alone who determines if there is a dividing line between yourself and any other human being, American or otherwise, and you alone can end that division at any time. Try it. Access that place in your mind where you understand that those you identify as being from the "other side" are simply Americans, just like you.

The "other side" exists only in your mind. Period.

* * *

A Way of Life

How did we come to fear and loathe our fellow Americans to this degree? In the past few decades, the amount of news we consume has grown exponentially. We have not only increased the amount of *time* we spend consuming news; we have also vastly expanded our *methods* of consumption. From newspapers and television to podcasts, internet, social media . . . even screens displayed in elevators, airplanes, taxi cabs, and at the gas pump. It's everywhere. There seems to be no escape.

But isn't that a good thing? Knowledge is power, right? Well, even food—which we need to survive—can be dangerous in extreme quantities.

And, as with food, we each have our own unique tastes when it comes to news consumption, most often related to our political leanings. We are no longer limited to three networks and the local paper. We can *choose* how we receive our news from an endless array of delivery options, and from a vast selection of pundits. So we designate our favorites to preach to us—delivering the details of each story, sure, but also providing perspective, interpreting meaning, amplifying threats, and performing moral reasoning for us.

For far too many Americans, *politics is the new religion*, and these "preaching pundits" have become their modern-day pastors. In a chaotic world, they appear to offer concrete good versus evil answers, giving adherents a sense of control over the uncontrollable. A practical synonym for *religion* is *way of life*; and, for many people, politics has become their way of life, 24/7.

Just to clarify, I certainly do not mean to imply that politics is in any way divine or that it has replaced any relationship one may have with a higher power. I mean that we have become so dedicated to our politics—they have become so intertwined with our identities—that our party affiliations have metamorphosed into denominations. They have become part of who we are, and we are religiously faithful to them.

Each day, we rely on these pastors—television anchors, podcast personalities, radio show hosts, "YouTubers," and social media influencers — to act as our guides as the epic *party vs. party* battle unfolds before us. Each "side" with their own, larger-than-life "saviors" — the Donald Trumps and the Barack Obamas, the Mitch McConnells and the AOCs. We root for "our side" when it emerges from a skirmish victorious, and cry foul when the "other side" lands a blow. And no matter what atrocities "our side" might commit,

Politics in America is the binding secular religion.

THEODORE H. WHITE

we always have our pastors on hand to justify it all for us. To make us feel comfortable. To assure us that "our side" is undeniably in the right.

Most of us rarely stop to consider that, just *maybe*, "our side" carries a portion of the blame. To recognize fault by "our side" would be to diminish our very selves and shake the foundations on which we stand. We cling to the supremacy of "our" leaders as pillars of our own esteem and communal standing. It is the adult equivalent of *"my dad could beat up your dad."* We cannot admit any weakness or culpability on "our side," for to do so would be tantamount to blasphemy.

Daily, we are not only witnessing but *participating in* this "political soap opera." The drama is more riveting than a football game played against our most bitter rival, and more engrossing than a television series featuring the evilest of villains, because we feel as though we are *part of the fight.* We believe we are "fighting" for a just cause, and that without our support not only would our side lose but the country itself might cease to exist.

Social psychology tells us that our self-esteem is linked to the groups we belong to. We follow and root for our party not necessarily because we believe that its legislative agenda is best for America, but more because we feel better about ourselves when "our side" wins. When "our side" loses an election or legislative battle, we feel that America is losing its soul.

Our country has regular competitions for status—known as elections—and, when "our side" is involved, we become more active, informed, and emotionally responsive to winning and losing. We also become more biased against the "other side" and more likely to argue on social media or face to face.

This heightened state of tribal warfare is—unfortunately— no longer reserved for election cycles. Increasingly, legislation is being framed according to our tribal affiliation and positioned as a win or loss for "our side," leaving us feeling that we are continually fighting for status. A recent study from Northwestern found that, for the first time on record, people's contempt for the "other" party is now *greater* than their fondness for their own.[1b]

Welcome to the politics of hate.

Here is the hard, bitter truth: the "war" is *all in your head.* Your mind is the battlefield as well as what is at stake—not the "soul" of the country, as you may believe. Advertisers, media companies, personalities, politicians, parties, and attention-seekers are intentionally demonizing the "other side" to enrage you, to gain your attention. The greater your fear and outrage—and the more time you spend consuming their content—the more advertising they sell, the more you donate, and the more money you make for them.

And yes, they are doing it intentionally. They are creating "news" stories, talk radio programs, articles, memes, and podcasts that divide the country, and they are doing it to make money or advance their cause. *Period.*

If you hate half of America, you have become a pawn on someone else's chessboard.

* * *

We Need an Intervention

Human beings are naturally curious social animals, and our brains are voraciously hungry for knowledge. Evolutionarily speaking, having abundant information increased our chances of survival, so our dopamine neurons treat new data as a reward. We evolved to gossip as an intelligence-gathering technique—a means of tracking our community without having to physically see and experience everything ourselves. This is how we shared useful information, such as who is mating with whom, who did not contribute to the last hunt, etc.

In the modern world, gossip is always readily available. Our data-hungry minds can snack indiscriminately on both information and misinformation and cannot always distinguish between the two. Either way, our primitive brain receives a cognitive incentive. So, when we hear a story about the "other side," we accept it, whether the information is credible or not (especially if it confirms our opinions and beliefs). We collect a chemical reward if we see actual video footage of a politician saying something vile, or if someone merely tells us that they did. *Our ancient brains do a lousy job of distinguishing between a witnessed indiscretion and one we just "heard about."*

Whenever human behavior creates a dopamine response in the human brain, you will find addictive and painful societal consequences.

- *As food became cheap and abundant,*
  obesity increased.

- *As fossil fuels became cheap and abundant,*
  climate change took hold.

- *As consumer goods became cheap and abundant,*
  hoarding and wastefulness soared.

- *As alcohol, recreational drugs, gambling,*
  and video games became cheap and abundant,
  harmful addictions have skyrocketed.

With the rise of the internet and social media, *information has become cheap and abundant*, and we have seen a sharp

increase in misinformation, disinformation, conspiracy theories, and social and political upheaval.

Like the issues above, this problem will be hard to tackle—because if we enjoy the behavior, we will rationalize why it should continue unabated. Human beings love their dopamine, and we hate being told to curb our desires.

You've seen a film or television show in which a character becomes addicted and is given an intervention. How did that person respond? Most likely with denial, panic, resentment, outrage, and personal attacks.

The truth hurts.

You may have judgmentally thought, "That poor sonuhvagun; why can't they see their problem? That would never happen to me."

But can you honestly say that you are not addicted—at least in some measure—to fearing, demeaning, loathing, slandering, mocking, or smearing other Americans?

If not, *this is your intervention.*

* * *

Your Mind is a Battlefield

As humans, we are innately tribal. The roots of this stretch back to our ancient past, when our very survival was often dependent upon acceptance by—and protection of—a tribe, clan, or other societal community.

The instinct to favor, affiliate with, and fiercely protect one group remains with us to this day—and can warp our thinking. We might associate with and vehemently defend political parties to feed this archaic need. Consequently, these parties become our modern-day tribes, and any threat or triumph related to them might trigger our brain's powerful hormonal responses— releasing epinephrine, cortisol, and adrenaline to put us on high alert when we sense an attack, and pleasure-inducing dopamine when we claim a victory.

These resources are costly.

While the brain comprises only about 3% of the human body, it consumes 25% of our overall energy budget. Your thoughts are incredibly expensive, in biological terms. If you have ever wondered why following politics can feel simultaneously exhausting *and* exhilarating, it is due to this costly cycle of motivation, reward, and reinforcement.

**

A disciplined mind leads to happiness, and an undisciplined mind leads to suffering.

DALAI LAMA

It's a rollercoaster that taxes you both mentally and physically, which is why you can feel exhausted after a day of "news" consumption.

As much as we may imagine that the vehement protection of our party is admirable and necessary, it is *not*. And while categorizing those within our "tribe" as friends, and all others as foes, might have served us well in the ancient past, today it is contributing to a growing, dangerous polarization.

Even the world's biggest thrill-seekers cannot survive if their feet never hit solid ground. What could you save by simply exiting the ride? Remember: when you read, watch, or listen to political news, you are not just witnessing the battle, *your mind is the battlefield, and you are paying an extremely high price for it.*

* * *

Stupid
The ~~Second~~ ^ Civil War
IT'S ALL IN YOUR HEAD. LITERALLY.

In 1994, research showed that only 21% of Republicans held a "very unfavorable" view of Democrats, and, among Democrats, only 17% viewed Republicans "very unfavorably." Fast forward 22 years and those numbers had more than doubled, with 58% of Republicans viewing Democrats "very unfavorably," and 55% of Dems holding a "very unfavorable" attitude about the GOP. (After five of the most socially and politically fractious years in American history, I would be willing to wager those numbers have now increased to 75% or more.)[1c]

What else has grown exponentially since 1994? Not just the *amount* of news we consume, but also the media's penchant for turning those on the "other side" into *exaggerated, mockable caricatures* based on extremes and fringes. As a result, we now radically misperceive those affiliated with "other" parties, and we have erroneously come to believe that there is no common ground to be found. But here is the less entertaining—and less marketable—truth: there really is more that unites us than divides us.

We are fighting an enemy that does not exist because peace is less profitable.

We agree on much more than we might realize. There is an astonishing (and expanding) perception gap between what we *imagine* the "other" party wants and what they really, genuinely believe. In short, your political adversaries aren't nearly as radical as you might suppose. Consider the following statistics from a 2019 "More in Common" poll (www.perceptiongap.us)[1d]

- *Immigration*
  Democrats estimated that only about half of Republicans would say properly controlled immigration was good for America. The actual number? Over 80%.
  Perception Gap = 33%

- *Police*
  Republicans believed that less than half of Democrats polled would *disagree* that "all police are bad."
  In truth, more than 80% opposed that statement.
  Perception Gap = 37%

These are just a couple of examples of how wrong we can be about the "other side." We agree on more than most of us realize....

- **Gun Control.** Those on the left often believe that those on the right are opposed to all forms of gun restrictions. But according to research, 79% of Republican or Republican-leaning respondents are in favor of background checks for private sales and at gun shows,

15

83% believe those on a federal watch or "no-fly" list should be barred from purchasing firearms, and 89% are in favor of preventing those with mental illnesses from purchasing guns (the same percentage as Democrats or those who lean Democrat).[1e]

- **Clean Energy.** It's not just for the far left. A 2018 survey showed that 79% of Republican or Republican-leaning respondents favored increasing wind turbine farms, and 84% supported increasing solar farms. In 2020, 88% favored a proposal to plant about a trillion trees to absorb carbon emissions.[1f, 1g]

- **Trade.** 68% of Republicans and 71% of Democrats polled in 2014 agreed that "trade is good." What else did they agree on? That it does not create jobs (only 24% of Republicans and 19% of Democrats felt that it did). That's only a 3% and a 5% gap, respectively.[1h]

- **Education.** Republicans, Democrats, and Independents seem to agree on the need for education reform. 65%, 67%, and 67%, respectively, felt the program was in need of rebuilding or major policy changes.[1i]

- **Elected Officials.** Americans of both major parties are united in their *distrust* of those who are elected to office. Only 36% of Democrats and 37% of Republicans claim to have a "great deal/fair amount of confidence in" elected officials.[1j]

Americans stand united on many issues, as illustrated in the charts that follow:

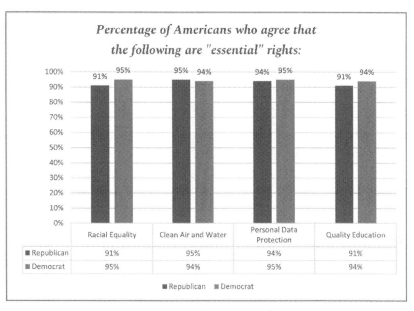

Source: Harvard Kennedy School,
Carr Center for Human Rights Policy, 2020[1k]

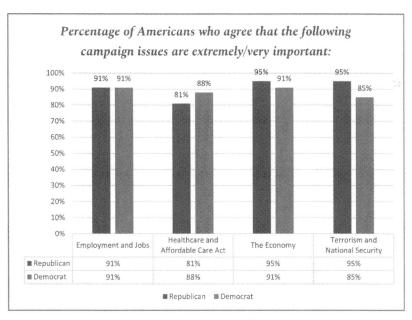

Source: Gallup, 2016[1l]

17

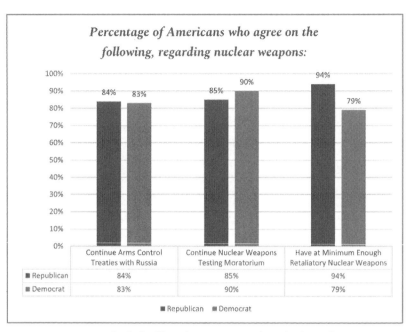

Percentage of Americans who agree on the following, regarding nuclear weapons:

	Continue Arms Control Treaties with Russia	Continue Nuclear Weapons Testing Moratorium	Have at Minimum Enough Retaliatory Nuclear Weapons
Republican	84%	85%	94%
Democrat	83%	90%	79%

Source: School of Public Policy, University of Maryland, 2020[lm]

This is not to say that we agree on everything—far from it. I am only including examples here of where we mostly see eye-to-eye, and I fully admit that. There is plenty we disagree on, but my point is that we have much more in common than we may realize, and we should not allow different points of view to divide us so severely. We do not need to be "the same" or hold the same beliefs to cooperate or enjoy a cohesive community.

We are hard-wired to look for similarities between ourselves and our fellow humans. But we do not merely celebrate them, we often use them as reasons to *exclude* other people. We learn to trust people who are like us, which makes us want everyone around us to be like us. In turn, people who are not like us may seem suspicious or even unlikeable. We judge them, and fool ourselves into thinking they are unpleasant, uneducated; or, even worse, we convince ourselves that we cannot coexist with them. But partisan shunning, shaming, and intolerance cost us dearly, and in more ways than we might realize.

Judgmentalism is a false promise. Although disguised as a pathway to social superiority, it is one of the most proven pathways to emotional rot, and judgmental people are among the loneliest and least happy on the planet. *When we judge, we are committing an act of intolerance, arrogantly labeling ourselves as superior, and dividing ourselves from others.*

* * *

Why You're Here

The simple fact that you have picked up and begun to read this book signifies that you recognize there is a problem. You have felt it, you have witnessed it, perhaps you're even part of it. And you know it's only going to escalate without a concerted effort to solve it.

Perhaps you've similarly experienced losing friends, family, or coworkers (shunning). It could be that you have had the experience of being outed in public (doxing). Maybe you've struggled in your personal relationships or your dating life, or you've questioned how to engage with others of differing views on social media. You may have grappled with hurt feelings, anger, rage, depression, anxiety, held a grudge against someone, or looked back with remorse on now-broken relationships and been unsure how to go about repairing them. The damage feels too great, and the divide insurmountable.

You are far from alone.

I've seen examples of these feelings everywhere in the past several years, through my speaking and training work, as well as in my personal life: unfriending, blocking, broken relationships, broken homes, lost jobs, a feeling of hopelessness...

The division is extreme. There's a perceived pressure to shame others to retain one's place in a community. Far too many Americans are focused on figuring out how to bludgeon the "other side" into submission, or devising schemes to help their "side" win while inflicting maximum pain and damage. Some are consumed by thoughts of figuratively (and sometimes literally) annihilating half the country. We've arrived at a point where otherwise seemingly well-adjusted, intelligent people have made startling declarations, such as *"If I could put a gun to the head of every person (from the opposing political party), I would."*

Some people place *so much value* on political differences, they imagine the world would be a better place if they didn't have to deal with another political party at all. Add to all this the increase in violence, riots, deaths, and hate crimes across the country, and it becomes obvious that **we've got a real problem on our hands.**

> ❝
> *Hate is poison and ultimately those who hate poison themselves.*
>
> ANITA LASKER-WALLFISCH

- *Shunning people from our communities*

- *Shaming them for their behavior*
- *Casting out family members*
- *Limiting our contact*
- *Spending too much time in the comments section*
- *"Doom scrolling" the news*

...none of this is helping.

On both the micro (personal) and macro (national) level, we're no longer able to come to a consensus, on matters political *or* personal, and it's rapidly eroding our ability to coexist or survive as a nation.

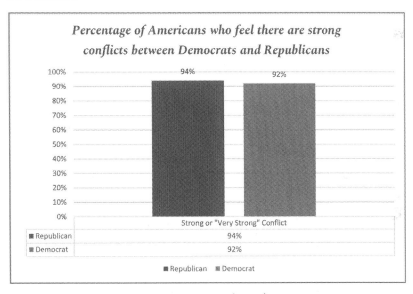

Source: Pew Research, 2020[10]

We're careening rapidly toward a no-win war that might very well lead to the destruction of our country.

By focusing on differences and alienating ourselves from those we disagree with, we not only push them further into their ineffective ideological hole, but we also make cooperation impossible. *No one can win this way.*

Our species rose to the top of the natural order because of our ability to cooperate: to unify and complete tasks that contribute to a common goal. The way I see it, there are no more important questions we can ask ourselves, as humans, than:

- *How can we cooperate better to solve our collective problems?*

- *How can we work together to move this country, and the world, forward?*

- *How can we just get along?*

You might think this is a Political Science, Sociology, or Psychology book, and yes—those elements are present. But this is a *self-leadership* book that provides practical steps anyone can implement, not only to make their lives better and improve their relationships but also to heal our nation.

Change starts with you.

If you picked up this book thinking you were just going to sharpen your partisan ax, you chose the wrong book. If you thought it would help you

Everyone thinks of changing the world, but no one thinks of changing himself.

LEO TOLSTOY

point the finger at the "other side" and prove just how wrong they are, you're sorely mistaken. If you bought this book to identify ways that "others" should change, it's time to get real.

This is a book about improving your life, and that doesn't happen by someone else changing. Once you've empowered yourself, you will be able to empower others to do the same.

The tools you will find within this book, if implemented, will have a profound and positive impact on . . .

- *Your personal and working relationships*
- *Your social media and news consumption*
- *Your patriotism*

...steering you away from the common enemies of rage, misinformation, and fear; leading you instead toward positive change; and helping you to experience . . .

- *Improved relationships*
- *More mindful and meaningful social media use*
- *Healthier news consumption*
- *Increased positive patriotism*
- *An improved social climate for everyone*

All you must do is decide
to take that *first step.*

Antebellum

"The city seemed to be perfectly frantic with delight. I never in all my life witnessed such excitement."

CITIZEN OF VIRGINIA - APRIL, 1861

Describing celebrations in the South related to the fall of Fort Sumter, leading up to a declaration of secession that would usher in the Civil War—and the deaths of 620,000 Americans

CHAPTER TWO

THE HIGH PRICE OF CIVIL WAR

*"It is painful enough to discover
with what unconcern they speak of war
and threaten it. They do not know its horrors.
I have seen enough of it to make me look
upon it as the sum of all evils."*

THOMAS JONATHAN "STONEWALL" JACKSON
American Civil War Confederate General

O n January 6, 2021, a mob of angered American citizens stormed the United States Capitol Building in Washington, D.C. As I am writing these words it is still relatively recent news, but I would imagine that, even if you are reading this book long after its initial publication, the events of that day remain quite vivid in your mind. Even citizens who shared the core concerns of the rioters were shaken by the events of that day. It was an aggressive display of political hostility and an act of domestic terrorism.

I was nearing completion of the writing of this book when those events took place. I, like so many others, had already seen the division festering and had worried that it might soon boil over. Some argued that another fully realized civil war in the United States was unlikely—that there was not enough at stake politically or socially to motivate it. I wanted to believe that was true. I wanted to be wrong about this. But, for me, January 6th was a chilling confirmation of my worst fears, and a loud warning shot across the bow.

History has a nasty habit of repeating itself. The further away an event is, the easier it becomes for us to say things like "sure, back *then*, but that could never happen *now*." But that kind of thinking is equal parts arrogant and hazardous. Are we so much wiser than our predecessors? Are things really all that different?

Historians argue about the myriad causes of the American Civil War of 1861. But while many things contributed to that sad chapter in American history, the issue of slavery was undisputedly front and center. That fact is the sticking point for some. That is, they feel the "temperature" is much cooler now because the issues of today don't have the same weight and significance as that of slavery. While I certainly won't claim that our modern-day issues carry identical importance to that of the abolitionist movement, let's look at them collectively: racism, equality, gun laws, privacy, the role of government; these are, in fact, very weighty issues. Perhaps the "climate" today isn't all that different, after all?

Division is alive and well, unfortunately, and, just like in early 1861, many desire a large-scale conflict. They believe it's the salve that will heal our nation. They've imagined themselves as righteous warriors. They've glorified it in their minds.

They've wished for it.

If you still believe that a modern-day American civil war is not possible, I challenge you to look more closely. I believe the seeds have already been planted, and they're beginning to take root.

* * *

What is a Civil War, and How Bad Would It Be?

Put simply, a *civil war* is a violent conflict between regions or political factions within the same state, territory, or country. Political and historical scholars have defined it as an armed conflict within a country that reaches more than 1,000 deaths in a given year. These internal hostilities are ruinous for economies, government institutions, environments, and the health and well-being of anyone caught up in them, whether by choice or by circumstance.

The greatest curse that can befall a free people, is civil war.

ALEXANDER H. STEPHENS

Wars can be either *hot* or *cold*. A "hot" civil war is physically violent, with weapons ranging from guns, grenades, and missiles to knives, clubs, and baseball bats. A "cold" civil war begins without physical violence but may "heat up" as tensions escalate.

There's no similar measure to determine at what point a cold war has begun or identify the moment at which we graduate from mere disagreement to doing battle. We are currently in a painful cold war; and while a cold civil war might not feature large-scale military conflict, make no mistake—it is very damaging. Even those of us not actively fighting can be caught up in it, resulting in increased anxiety, fear, and extreme fatigue.

All human cooperation is based on a shared agreement as to what is factual, so it's not surprising that we cannot seem to locate common ground these days. It's difficult to know what to believe, and some of that, unfortunately, is by design. Propaganda and "whisper campaigns" run rampant, while fake social media profiles and news websites lurk around every corner. We're bombarded with a steady and conflicting stream of both fact and misinformation that we must actively sort through and critically examine to the point of exhaustion. This side wants you to hate that side. That side wants you to hate this side. We've seen shaming (online mocking, humiliation), shunning (unfriending, blocking, distancing), doxing (sharing confidential information publicly), and intimidation (threats of harm).

We are unquestionably in a cold civil war. *And the temperature is rising.*

I often wondered what a new American Civil War might look like. On January 6th of this year, we got a sneak preview. Sadly, it was just the latest in an extensive list of violent incidents I've witnessed in recent months, including hate crimes, abuse of power, riots, and assaults based on race, ethnicity, occupation, and political affiliation. This is a pattern commonly seen in an internalized cold war, along with significant shifts in the economy and leadership.

* * *

The closer something is to us—in terms of time, interest, or geography—the more invested we feel, and the greater impact it can have. This is our flawed moral reasoning, which also prioritizes good acts over good intentions and physically violent events (such as a terrorist attack) over those that are physically invisible (such as a pandemic).

Conflicts that are recent, like the Rwandan Civil War or the Yugoslav Wars, feel "real" in a way that ancient events do not—and we're far more aware of the graphic details. And so, while they might not be perfectly comparable in terms of their causes and provocations, I will point to these to illustrate just how dangerous our current trajectory could be.

Though the war in Rwanda was focused on the state of rule and in Yugoslavia on religion, both saw friend turn against friend, and neighbor against neighbor, in favor of a cause they felt was more important than their shared communities. The result? Approximately 140,000 people died in the Yugoslav Wars, with entire towns abandoned or destroyed. In Rwanda, the conflict sparked genocide, which resulted in the slaughter of approximately 800,000 people. [2a, 2b]

Could this happen in the United States? I'm sure we would all like to believe that it couldn't, but the hard truth is—it absolutely could. Both tragic examples above began without violence and eventually escalated. Both began with disagreements and ended in bloodshed. It would be arrogant and pretentious of us to imagine that we would never find ourselves in a comparable situation.

It has happened before.

Our American Civil War resulted in more than 620,000 military casualties and an estimated 50,000 civilian deaths. That's about 2.13% of the population. If we lost the same percentage of U.S. citizens today, the death toll would be nearly 7 million people. [2c]

Imagine losing 7 million people.

Try to picture that for a moment. I don't mean to be morbid, it's just that we tend to look at data as just that. We must be mindful that these aren't merely numbers on a page, they represent human beings. Real people who, like us and those we love, had thoughts, ideas, interests, loves, and *value.*

If I handed you seven pieces of paper and asked you to toss them into a fire, could you do it? Could you watch them burn? It would not be a problem for you. But what if you looked down and noticed that those pieces of paper were $100 bills? At this point, you might ask me *why* I wanted you to do it. After all, if my reason resonated with you, you might be on board. Now imagine it was *seventy thousand* $100 bills.

In all three scenarios, you were asked to throw fuel onto a fire. The only difference was in the value *you* placed on what would be lost in the process. Unfortunately, we're not always fully able to see the price that will be paid, and even when we do see it we might not care . . . so long as we don't think we'll be stuck with the bill.

Americans are throwing fuel onto a dangerous fire because it costs them truly little. There is currently no pressing, quantifiable price to be paid. If you were able to see a direct connection between your words and actions, and the deaths of human beings, you would absolutely change them.

I'm telling you now, unequivocally, that when we participate in the growing political divide, even in insignificant ways, there is a very real cost.

Those in favor of war—those who believe in its necessity and effectiveness—often attempt to glorify their cause, promising that participants will be lauded as heroes, painting a beautiful picture of the utopia that awaits on the other side of an easy victory, and assuring us that we'll all win in the end.

Nothing could be further from the truth. The cost of war will always far outweigh any potential gains. We pay dearly, and the price is economic, cultural, and human.

> **"**
>
> *The folly of war is that it can have no natural end except in the extinction an entire people.*
>
> JOYCE CAROL OATES

In war, there are no winners. Only those who lose less.

CHAPTER THREE

HOW SEVERE IS YOUR CIVIL WAR?

"There is a savage beast in every man,
and when you hand that man a sword or spear
and send him forth to war, the beast stirs."

GEORGE R.R. MARTIN

A Storm of Swords

A s humans, we have an inherent need to be right. We manifest that need through correcting others, which often leads to heated discussions, arguments, fractured relationships. But sometimes it goes beyond that, causing physical confrontations, rioting, destruction, and even death.

Defending our beliefs is something we all do, and it is crucial to our emotional and physical survival. Some *methods are more acceptable than others.*

On the extreme side of things, physically harming someone based on their beliefs is not acceptable. Dismissing an employee because of their views is certainly not okay. But less extreme practices, such as ridiculing someone on social media and trolling them in the comments section, are also inappropriate. These actions are ineffective and only further our divide. They do not help. They do not heal.

Civil discussions—in which everyone has an opportunity to share their thoughts without fear of judgment or ridicule—must be the goal.

We have *all* failed in the quest to promote and participate in peaceful conversations. (Some more than others.) Those who do not worry themselves with the political landscape might be accused of contributing to the problem by way of their complacency. But those on the opposite end of the spectrum— who regularly utilize social media channels to promote and provoke—are a part of the problem as well. They are a much *larger* part, as their divisive posts, comments, and tactics are collectively increasing the "temperature."

Can we avoid a civil war? Is there any way to cool things down and recover from this hazardous polarization? *Yes.* But it will require each of us, individually, to *recognize* what our contributions have been, *accept* the role we have played, and be *genuinely willing* to change our own behaviors.

* * *

This Time, It's Personal

One of the major differences between civil wars of the past and the one we're now headed toward is that this one is very personal. While the wars of the 20th century were waged by countries or institutions, the rise of unethical media, combined with the now universally accessible power of technology, has placed us, as individuals, both on the front lines and within the command bunkers. **We are not just fighting the war, *we are running it.***

It's personal. It isn't region versus region, race versus race, or even "haves" versus "have nots." The "sides" in this war are based on political affiliation, and that's a major difference because our political views are opinion-based. *Personal.* You're not born into them (well, not inescapably)— they're in your control. So unlike some conflicts in which you will automatically find most of your friends, neighbors, and loved ones

> *There is a huge amount of freedom that comes to you when you take nothing personally.*
>
> DON MIGUEL RUIZ

in your corner, this war is pitting parent against child, spouse against spouse, neighbor against neighbor. One half of the country wanting to obliterate the other is bad enough, but when they're willing to do it *knowing* that friends, neighbors, and family will be lost in the process . . . that's unusually terrifying. Whether or not we wanted it, this war is *mine* and this war is *yours.*

Your war is not (yet) being fought with guns or swords, but with shaming, shunning, and other "emotional" weapons, leading to the dangerous cancel culture we now inhabit. What began with subtle derision soon escalated beyond mocking and ridicule to include doxing, unfriending, empathy denial, intimidation, and even death threats. Which of these have you participated in? How far has it gone?

It may be uncomfortable to look at the role you've played, and difficult to recognize all the ways in which you've directly (or indirectly) contributed, but you must. *We all must.* It's important work, and every individual who undertakes that work will play a pivotal role in deescalating the mounting threat to our country.

* * *

Evaluating (and Ending) Your War

The goal of this book is to act as a handbook—guiding you toward correcting conflict-contributing behaviors and ending your personal civil war. (Hopefully, at this point you feel I've made a good case as to why this work is important.) To that end, please answer the questions that follow.

*If you prefer, visit **www.SecondCivilWar.co** to take this quiz online ("How Severe is Your Civil War") and your answers will be automatically calculated.*

1. How important are politics to you?

___ *I don't follow politics and don't know many people's names.*

___ *I only know the political highlights or most major events.*

___ *I feel informed and up-to-date most of the time.*

___ *I feel staying informed is necessary, obligatory.*

___ *I feel it is obligatory, and I know every important detail.*

2. How much time do you spend catching up on news, daily?

_____

Include television, newspapers, websites, etc. (Some of this data can be researched on your computer or phone.)

3. How much time do you spend on social media, daily?

_____

Scrolling through your feed, posting, watching videos, reading comments, etc. Be sure to think about all the social media channels/platforms you may use (Facebook, Twitter, Instagram, etc.)

4. In total, how many of your daily waking hours are spent thinking about or consuming news about politics?

_____

5. On a scale of 1-10, how angry are you at "the other side"?

(NOT ANGRY) 1 2 3 4 5 6 7 8 9 10 *(VERY ANGRY)*

6. Do you feel you're having more of a *positive* or a *negative* impact on those around you?

_____

Are you changing lives, making them worse, or simply existing?

Each of the questions you just answered corresponds with a category (column) on the following chart. Look back at your responses, then, under each chart category, circle the "phase" (row) that best matches your answer:

CATEGORIES

		Political Priority QUESTIONS 1-2	Engagement w/News & Social Media QUESTIONS 2-3	Common Behaviors QUESTION 4	Common Emotions QUESTION 5	Social Impact QUESTION 6
PHASE 1	*Totally unaware*	May or may not vote. No strong feelings about political parties or who is in office.	May use social media to connect, but keeping up with news is not a priority.	Simple routine of work, relationships, etc.	Relaxed. Busy with other things. Passive.	No measurable impact on others. Passive. May be perceived as complacent.
PHASE 2	*Occasionally up-to-date*	Probably votes. Knows the names of a few important figures in Congress. Reads major headlines.	Uses social media to connect and may read stories others share. Only looks at news on occasion or for headlines.	Simple routine of work, relationships, etc. Only occasionally interacts with the news.	Relaxed. Busy with other things. Passive. Calm regarding the news.	Minimal impact on others. Passive. May be perceived as complacent.
PHASE 3	*Angry and anxious (sometimes)*	Votes. Has a firm opinion of their political affiliation. Moderately up-to-date on the news.	Uses social media often, reads articles, engages on subjects they're concerned about. Strong opinions about some subjects.	Frequently uses social media. Sometimes argues in comments. Some opinionated posts or articles. Likely doesn't fact-check.	Angry/anxious about subjects they deeply care about. Passive about others. May struggle with bouts of anger, sadness, or anxiety.	Negative impact when they don't fact-check or argue. May be considered complacent in the subjects they disregard.
PHASE 4	*At wits' end*	Votes. Has a firm opinion of their political party and those not affiliated with it. Always up-to-date on the news.	At least a few hours per week spent on social media, reads others' political posts and news, and shares. Gets in trouble in the comments or trolls others.	Frequent use of social media and news. Burdened relationships. Shares opinionated posts or articles without fact-checking.	Actively struggles with rage, sadness, or anxiety. Wishes they could take a break from it all, but feels a responsibility to stay connected, informed.	Negative impact frequently. Hurt relationships. Overly opinionated. May be blindly loyal to political party.
PHASE 5	*Trench warfare*	Strong opinions about party, votes for it no matter what, judgmental or hateful of others. Up-to-date on every news detail, immediately.	Hours on social media daily, reads articles, posts, shares, and argues with others. Far too much news consumed. May attend protests, rallies, etc.	Hours daily on social media, or watching and reading news. Trolls others, argues in the comments. Shares articles and conspiracies w/o fact-check.	Lives with hopelessness, sadness, and rage. Increased anxiety and depression. Obsessive. May visualize acts of violence.	Negative. Hatred. Closed minded. False information. Bias. Overly opinionated or blindly loyal.

Now review where your circled responses fell. All your circles should appear on the same horizontal line (the same "phase" row), but there may be one or two outliers. **The phase where you have the most circles is your** *predominant phase.*

As an example, say someone is extremely interested in the news and argues frequently with others about politics, but they do not use social media. This would place them in *Phase 4* or *Phase 5*, depending on the intensity.

If you are split between two phases, it may indicate that you are in a transition period. You may be feeling more vulnerable than usual, or fitting more social media or news viewing time into your schedule. Ask yourself what might have caused this change and how you might address it to make yourself feel calmer and safer. *(I will try to help with that, too.)*

Note your predominant phase(s), and read on....

* * *

How Severe is Your Civil War?

Now that you've identified what phase (or phases) you're in, let's take a closer look at what each phase means, and where/how you might make improvements.

Note: The phase explanations below are generalizations, of course, and you may not feel the description I've provided is a perfect fit. But hopefully it's close enough that you can find something of use.

Predominant phase:

TOTALLY UNAWARE

"Where ignorance is bliss, 'tis folly to be wise."

THOMAS GRAY

You're minimally involved in the political landscape. You're not caught up in the political shifting of the nation. When others were in a panic or elated based on whether Joe Biden or Donald Trump was president, there's a good chance you felt extraordinarily little about the whole thing. No doubt you heard about issues in and around the year 2020—impeachment trials, Black Lives Matter, the insurrection—but this news primarily came to you by word of mouth or a simple scanning of the headlines. You remained unaware of the finer details.

You're not wrong for living this way. There's a certain charm to keeping a distance from politics. However, as a citizen of the United States, it is your responsibility to participate in our democracy by voting—and to do that well and wisely, you do need to have a working knowledge of the news.

I would recommend that you aim to review the headlines once each week, or even biweekly, so you have a sense of what's going on in the nation and around the world, one that is not contaminated by the misinformation or opinion that can seep into even well-intentioned word-of-mouth news. Also, be sure to research who your elected representatives are so you will know whose office to reach out to if you ever want to help make change.

Predominant phase:

BARELY AWARE

"The dull pain of truth weights my soul,
pulling it under.
I am left hopelessly awake."

LIBBA BRAY

You're slightly more informed than those in the previous phase. You may ponder the headlines or read the occasional news article, but staying fully up-to-date on politics isn't a high priority for you.

Again, *there is nothing wrong with living this way,* but I will remind you, too, of the importance of your democratic duties. I would recommend getting into a routine of perusing news once a week, or biweekly, to stay on top of major events and to stay slightly more informed, more often. And, of course, make a point to be aware of who your elected representatives are (if you don't already) so you will know whose office to reach out to if you ever want to help make change.

Frankly, I fall into this category myself . . . and some days I wish I was *"Totally Unaware."* I find it takes discipline not to submit to the temptation of increasing my news consumption and falling into the "Anxious and Angry" category.

Predominant phase:

ANXIOUS AND ANGRY (SOMETIMES)

*"Many of us crucify ourselves between two thieves—
regret for the past and fear of the future."*

FULTON OURSLER

Perusing the news and social media is not all you do, far from it, but when a topic that's especially important to you is being discussed? You're front and center for as long as it takes.

This can be a slippery slope.

When you're in this phase, you're on the cusp (*of what* is up to you). You can either find a way to carefully pull back—just enough so that you remain well-informed but less emotionally invested—or you can get more deeply involved, which runs the risk of (among other things) damaging your relationships.

Take a moment to think about the subjects that upset you or excite you. How do you respond when you see someone talking about them?

- *Do you stay on social media and watch conversations?*
- *Do you obsess over news headlines?*
- *Do you comment or get into arguments?*
- *Do these developments and exchanges make you uncomfortable?*

Know what subjects impassion you, and feel free to support or challenge them. But it may be wise to reevaluate how much of your time and energy you're giving up in service of them.

You will also want to find the line between participation and provocation, and learn to tread it mindfully.

Predominant phase:

AT WITS' END

*"We drink the poison our minds pour for us
and wonder why we feel sick."*

ATTICUS

Society looks a little darker and a little more hopeless for you than it did a few years ago. You weren't always so invested in the news or social media, but these days you're discovering more and more issues that you "just can't take" anymore. You may also find that there's a growing list of topics you can't talk about with anyone who isn't on "your side" of a given issue.

Worse, you've begun to see the impact of this in your personal or professional life. Maybe you argued with a friend over politics and felt that you had to block them due to the things they were saying. Maybe *they* blocked *you*. Maybe you're markedly less productive at work because you're spending so much time doing other things online (tracking news stories, "doom scrolling," etc.)

You have some *very* strong opinions—perhaps stronger now than you recall them having been a few years ago. You may look at people differently these days (especially those you see on the news or in the office, or who have different views than you do). You're probably not sure how to stop any of this, and there's a good chance you don't (yet) want to. You might genuinely feel that what you're doing is helping.

I have bad news for you: what you're doing isn't helping at all. In fact, all you're really doing is separating yourself from others and encouraging divides between groups. There are other healthier, more positive ways to accomplish the change you want to see in this world.

Predominant phase:

TRENCH WARFARE

"Hell is empty and all the devils are here."

WILLIAM SHAKESPEARE

You've got a hair-trigger temper. You're an unpinned grenade—a lit Molotov cocktail primed to inflict emotional or physical suffering on any "traitor" from the "other side." You passionately believe that you stand on the side of righteousness....

...So why are you experiencing feelings of desperation, isolation, hurt, anger, anxiousness, unrest, and insatiable rage? And why does it feel both exhilarating and toxic at the same time?

You have divided yourself from people, and you've encouraged divisions between groups. You've changed the look and feel of your life by focusing less on personal interactions, work, and living, and more on obsessing over politics.

It's time to stop and realize there's another way to do this.

You can still make change in the world and good, positive change at that. But there is a better way to do it. You must strike a balance between this and other areas of your life, and repair those relationships I'm certain you've lost along the way.

CHAPTER FOUR

HOW DID WE GET HERE?

"If you spend time with crazy and dangerous people, remember—their personalities are socially transmitted diseases; like water poured into a container, most of us eventually turn into whoever we surround ourselves with."

STEFAN MOLYNEUX
Canadian Podcaster

O ne of the easiest ways to unify people is to rally them against a common enemy—real, imagined, or invented. Find a group of outsiders to vilify, point at them, and scream: *They want to take from you!* It is frighteningly simple, highly effective, and **incredibly destructive to humanity.**

If you've fallen victim to this, (and let's face it, we all have at some point), did it feel almost automatic or even instinctual? There is a reason for that. Tribalism—fierce loyalty to one's social group or "tribe"—is a behavior that is encoded in us. The impulse to protect one's own particular "group" is one of the most basic instincts, among humans and all social mammals.

While tribalistic instincts can get us into trouble, especially when manipulated, there are sound psychological and evolutionary reasons for their existence. In the ancient past, we banded together in small family groups and communities, and our survival was dependent upon their strength and endurance. Protecting the "tribe" was crucial. And so to this day our bodies release hormones such as testosterone and oxytocin, when necessary, to reinforce our tribal instincts and protect vital social cohesion.

The existence of these instincts is certainly no secret. The theme of heroically protecting family or community against a terrible foe is popular in literature, film, and television because it speaks to a universal desire and touches on our common fears. But while film producers and authors may trigger our ancient impulses as a means of creating more compelling entertainment, others who activate them are less well-intentioned.

The tribal instinct serves us well but leaves us quite vulnerable at the same time.

* * *

Basic Instinct: Cancel Culture

Expel the outsider. Banish the foreigner. Dread the stranger. This programming is the ancient ancestor of modern-day *cancel culture* . . . and the roots run deep.

Thousands of years ago, when our species lived in small groups, clans, or tribes, each person in that close-knit community played a significant role. Resourcefulness and reliability were essential to survival, as were cooperation, loyalty, and trust. Without these key characteristics, the community would crumble, and its members would eventually perish. So when a member fell out of line, the consequences were swift and severe.

Violations and undesirable behavior were dealt with by the offending member being called out (shamed) and often physically cast out (shunned). Without the protection and shared resources of a community, they would most likely starve, be killed by a predator, or fall victim to the elements. This was our earliest and most primal use of shaming and shunning, but these behaviors have continued to evolve with our species.

Americans now live with advanced technologies, and most have access to shelter, food, and clean water on a regular basis. Our needs have shifted. We no longer need to huddle together before sundown. We can now decide for ourselves, from the privacy of our homes, whether we wish to interact with our neighbors, family members, or friends.

Our use of shaming and shunning has transformed, as well, shifting mostly away from physical consequences in favor of verbal and emotional repercussions. Social media is often the delivery method of choice for those who inflict these punishments; their arsenal includes ridicule, gossip, and other abusive tactics.

Doxing, for example, has become an increasingly prevalent (and dangerous) form of abuse. This is when someone publicly reveals another's private or identifying information—with harmful intent. The perpetrator can carry out this vicious act from the comfort of their own home, believing that they carry little blame for the result as they are merely unleashing a *means* to harm and not the harm itself. They are activating an online army to do their "dirty work." It is a particularly heinous act of shaming and intimidation that often carries legal ramifications.

Shaming does not work. It is as cruel as it is ineffective, and counterproductive because shame triggers a defensive reaction. Think about it: has your behavior ever changed *positively* because of your having been insulted or teased? More likely you became angry. You may have even entertained notions of revenge. Shame does not alter behavior; it merely exacerbates it.

Shame did work as an effective tool to change your fellow tribesman's behavior 10,000 years ago because if you expelled them from the tribe, they would certainly die. Either they could not find enough food, get sick, injured, attacked by a foreign tribe or animal, or sustain an injury. Today, if you shame someone of "the other" political party, they just think, "What a jerk—thankfully, I have 75 million people (about twice the population of California) who approve of me."

> **"**
>
> *When you judge another, you do not define them, you define yourself.*
>
> WAYNE DYER

In terms of *shunning*, these days instead of casting someone out of our community in a physical sense, we are more likely to simply end our relationship with them. *Cancel culture* is the modern-day equivalent of ancient tribal banishment philosophy. It describes the pattern of withdrawing support from, ostracizing, censoring, and essentially "casting out" those whose actions or opinions we deem to be offensive and in direct conflict with our own. "Unfriending" and "blocking" are some of the most used contemporary cancellation tools—a means of removing and discarding someone from our lives and personal circles. Essentially, exiling them.

While there are certainly times when it's acceptable or even advisable to limit one's contact with someone else, especially if doing so may prevent you from harm, these days "cancellation" is becoming increasingly frequent, and with far less reason, provocation, or thought.

Our continued use of shunning techniques can be explained by the concept of *Evolutionary Mismatching*. Humans evolved based on, and adapted to, our ancient environment. In our modern world, those adaptations can "misfire." Simply put, we are still instinctively exhibiting behavior that worked for us thousands of years ago, despite it having a negative impact on us today. We are seeing an increase in damaged or broken relationships, with more impulsive endings. That is troubling enough on a personal level, but when we look at it through a wider lens, it becomes even more disturbing.

When we "cancel" someone from our own lives, we may think that this has a negligible impact outside of the two people involved. But when our reasons for "cancellation" are political, our actions radiate outward, contributing to the growing divide within our nation. *The small weight of our actions, when combined with those of so many others, becomes a crushing, unsustainable burden—capable of bringing about the literal collapse of our nation.*

More social media users are choosing to exclude, quickly and unceremoniously, those who do not share their political beliefs. Many have begun to view differently affiliated people as "others" or, sometimes, hardly as human at all. We're seeing a dramatic increase in hate crimes, racist and sexist commentary, riots, and general violence due to our intense focus on our differences and our refusal to seek out opportunities for cooperation.

Have you consciously "canceled" or limited contact with friends or family members due to political differences? Have you "unfriended," "unfollowed," or "blocked" people on social media? If so, *you've enacted your own personal cancel culture.* You have de-platformed those people and their ideas from the town hall of your mind. You've created a mental "safe space" where only supporting and confirming ideas reside—free of outside challenge. While this may seem blissfully serene, you have shut down your ability to understand that person, and shut down their ability to understand you. *You have deepened the divide and closed off all opportunities to make repairs.*

* * *

We Need a Hero

In the ancient past, in our small tribes, the person deemed most important was the leader. We may have looked to a higher power or deity of some kind, but we looked to the leader of our tribe as well, and this individual was similarly powerful and untouchable. They would have been perceived as more important, of higher stature and power, with more knowledge, skills, or wit than anyone else.

Following a designated leader carried ample benefits for our ancestors. But perceiving a leader in a too-gloriously-positive light—as if they can do no wrong—is blind *hero-worship*, which is extremely dangerous.

As I mentioned previously, for many, *politics is the new religion*. In recent years there has been a remarkable shift in our nation away from the idea of elected leaders as merely that, and toward a culture of leader-worship that is becoming, quite frankly, alarming. For some, allegiance to their leader of choice has become completely intertwined with their own identity. They may view an attack on that leader as an attack on their very selves and all that they hold dear. Worse, the greater their

Hero worship is demoralizing for the devotee and dangerous to the country.

DR. BABASAHEB AMBEDKAR

devotion becomes the less able they are to distinguish between fact and propaganda. They may reject what their deeper selves know to be true if they perceive it to be against their beliefs or find that it in any way diminishes their leader. For by the time they reach this point, to admit that their leader is fallible would be a form of self-harm.

If you want a textbook example of just how bad this has become, look no further than the Capitol insurrection on January 6, 2021. While not all those involved were violent, and certainly not all those who supported then-President Donald Trump condoned the actions of the insurrectionists (far from it), make no mistake: many of those involved were clearly, recklessly, engaging in *blind hero-worship*.

The danger of this can be illustrated through the words of their family members, many of whom spoke of how their loved ones had changed in recent days, months, and years—their identities so wrapped up in their support of then-President Trump that they had become almost unrecognizable. Alison Lopez was among many who turned in family members on discovering that they were part of the mob. "These are people who never really identified with politics before," she said, "and now they have just let this consume their lives."[4a]

On the day of the insurrection, one image stood out among the rest—that of the "QAnon Shaman," with his red, white, and blue painted face, bare chest, megaphone, fur, and horns.

It would be easy for us to look at those images and immediately assume that the man on the other end of them was a criminal with a history of violence. But he had no known criminal record at that time—he had not so much as been caught stealing a candy bar. Shortly after his arrest, there was "much ado" about his dietary requests, but aside from that reports indicate that he has been quiet, compliant, and helpful.

I do not say this to defend his actions or dismiss what he has done but to illustrate that blind hero-worship is not merely an affliction of the aggressive or disreputable. It can take hold of even the most peaceful among us and, once it has, wield tremendous power over our lives.

According to court records, this man believed that he had been called to action by then-President Donald Trump—that he had traveled to the District of Columbia *at the request of the president.* "It was a driving force by a man he hung his hat on, he hitched his wagon to," his attorney said. "He loved Trump. Every word, he listens to him." [4b, 4c]

He did listen. So much so that when he sat in Mike Pence's chair on the Senate floor, he referred to the then-Vice President as a *traitor* because he had refused to do Trump's bidding. Pence did not hold the legal power to overturn the results of the electoral college, but when Trump declared otherwise, his followers believed it—and acted.[4d]

And so, this self-proclaimed "shaman," who previously had no criminal record, became a symbol of one of the darkest days in American history, and he will forever be emblazoned in our memories as such.

But for his part? He has since expressed regret and disappointment. He claims the leader he so passionately followed "let a lot of peaceful people down." He has called the former president "dishonorable." He has asked that we be patient with him, and others like him, who are "having a very difficult time piecing together all that happened to us, around us, and by us." [4e, 4f]

It is likely that he had fully expected his beloved leader to defend and exonerate him, and he lost faith in a devastating way when he realized no one was coming to his rescue.

This disillusionment is reminiscent of the stories many of us read or watched as children—coming of age stories in which the main character finally meets their hero only to find that they're hardly heroic and could never live up to the idolized version of them the child had built up in their mind.

We need heroes. We need them so badly that we may cast an elected leader in the role, whether or not they belong there. We need them so badly we may then refuse to see that leader as being in any way fallible, creating for ourselves an almost super-human version of them that would be impossible to live up to.

Our elected leaders are public servants, not the other way around. So to cast them in the role of "hero" is a disservice to them as well as ourselves, and our country.

Democracy calls for us to be informed participants, making decisions that are in the best interest of our nation and our fellow citizens. We cannot fulfill our responsibility if we're hero worshipers who blindly follow and fiercely protect our leader no matter what. *We cannot fulfill our responsibility if we're only willing to act in the best interest of our perceived "teams."*

Imagine where the "shaman" would be today if he'd had a friend who told him that while it was okay to support the former President, it was okay not to agree with everything he did, and okay to question him, too. Imagine if he had listened. An open mind doesn't mean you have to give up your beliefs or principles; it simply means that you're willing to listen and consider other points of view. Your deeply-held values can withstand it, I promise you.

Consider asking a friend with a different political view for a conversation. Go into the conversation telling yourself (and them) that you are not there to defend or promote your opinion, only to listen to theirs. Then, listen intently to discover what it is they know that you don't, and why they feel the way they do. Ask thoughtful, kind questions to help you understand them. Try your best not to diminish their point of view. It may be difficult. It may feel uncomfortable. It may not change your mind one bit. But then again, *it just might be a life-changing conversation.*

When we allow different viewpoints and experiences into our lives, we give ourselves and others the opportunity to grow and (positively) change.

We didn't arrive at this place overnight, and we certainly can't fix it all overnight. But we can get started. You can get started—now. Today.

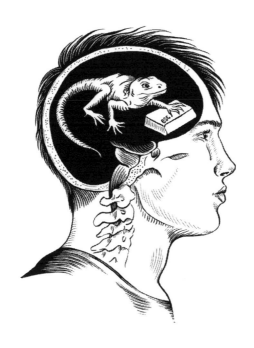

Personal Relationships:
Outsmart Your Lizard Brain

*"I never considered a difference
of opinion in politics, in religion,
in philosophy, as cause for
withdrawing from a friend."*

THOMAS JEFFERSON
*Lawyer, Philosopher, American Founding Father,
Statesman, Diplomat, and President (1801-1809)*

CHAPTER FIVE

ESCAPING
OUR TRIBALISM

"Tell me with whom you associate, and
I will tell you who you are."

JOHANN WOLFGANG VON GOETHE

Poet, Playwright, Novelist

I n terms of politics, *why* do you believe what you believe? Do
your views on topics such as taxes, immigration, the second
amendment, abortion, and the role of government spring
from your own mind? Have you formed your opinions based on
your own thoughtful study of what is in the best interest of our
country? Perhaps.

But probably not.

Most of us have good intentions, and we believe that our
views are right and true. We also believe that we have reached
that conclusion based on weighing our thoughts and values
against outcomes. That may be accurate, but the truth is that
our beliefs are often shaped by our ancient tribal instincts.

We believe to belong.

Picture this: through a modern-day mishap, you end up stranded on an uncharted island, desperate for food, water, shelter, and company. Just when you think you will surely starve or succumb to the elements, you discover that the island has other inhabitants—a primitive community that can provide everything you require. Assuming you were able to peacefully approach them, what would happen next?

It's highly likely that, over an extended period, you would end up adopting their language, dress, customs, and yes, even their beliefs. Why? Again, it's our ancient instinct at work. We crave acceptance and community to ensure our own survival.

Now perhaps you accept this idea, but you're thinking—*no, I'm sure that I could coexist without any meaningful change to who I am and what I believe.* You might find it difficult to imagine *how* anyone *could* make such a significant transition.

The answer is *assimilation*—another tool in our ancient arsenal. More than merely an outward show of conformity, assimilation is an internal process through which we slowly introduce current ideas and information to our existing knowledge, interpreting and rationalizing what we're learning along the way in a manner that helps it to "fit in" with our previously held notions. As we increasingly come to accept this new information, we eventually become absorbed into the dominant culture—in this case, the ways of the native islanders. This process can be unintentional and instinctive. Why? Because our ancient programming tells us that belonging is essential to assure our continued existence, and necessary to avoid shame, exclusion, or expulsion.

* * *

Tell Me With Whom You Associate and I Will Tell You What You Believe

The film "Dances With Wolves" offers us multiple examples of assimilation. Union Army Lieutenant John J. Dunbar (played by Kevin Costner) chooses a post on the edge of the colonized territories to see the frontier "before it's gone." Through a series of unfortunate events, Dunbar ends up alone and forgotten at Fort Sedgwick, which is deserted, dilapidated, and very remote.

Eventually, he comes into contact with members of the local Sioux tribe. The first encounters are hostile and tense, each side testing the measure of the other. But both Dunbar and the Sioux prove to be curious, empathetic, and patient—they do not allow hostile gestures to devolve into open violence.

Trust slowly builds between Dunbar and the Sioux as they begin a relational "dance." Dunbar is fascinated by the Sioux and their customs. He begins to learn their language in earnest, grows out his hair, and even adopts some of their dress. The Sioux invite him to join them for a sacred hunt, during which he saves the life of a young Sioux warrior—earning him even more trust and even a bit of "celebrity status" among the members of the tribe. When the tribe is attacked, Dunbar fights alongside Sioux warriors, demonstrating his devotion and allegiance. Ultimately, he abandons his post and marries a member of the tribe, and his inclusion is all but solidified.

Dunbar makes one final voyage to the fort to retrieve his journal, which contains a record of his journey. Spotted from afar, his transformed appearance leads Union Soldiers to believe that he is Native American—and they attack. Once captured, and despite providing his name and rank, Dunbar is shackled, beaten, interrogated, degraded, and treated with utter disrespect. At this point, his assimilation becomes complete, and he refuses to speak to them further, responding only in his new language and giving only his Sioux name, Dances With Wolves.

As he is being transported (to be tried and hung), members of his new tribe attack. They free Dances With Wolves, who joins them in killing the Union Soldiers— once and for all severing his former allegiances. His transformation into a member of the Sioux tribe is complete.

You are the only white man I have ever known. I have thought about you a lot. More than you think. And I understand your concern. But I think you are wrong. The white man the soldiers are looking for no longer exists. Now there is only a Sioux named Dances With Wolves.

TEN BEARS
Dances With Wolves, 1990

Not all assimilation is related to *literal* survival. Think of a high school student whose family moves from one part of the country to another. We've all been to high school. We know how important it is to fit in—somewhere, somehow—to "survive" those four years. The student would certainly learn and adapt to the new customs, mannerisms, and fashion of their classmates. If they were to return to visit their hometown a year or two later, their old friends might even tell them "you've changed!"

Whether or not we are acutely aware of it, we assimilate— even when we are not stranded on an uncharted island or wandering alone on the Great Plains. We learn to fit in with and take on the values and characteristics of our *community*—whatever or whomever that may be. These groups can be geographical, familial, religious, interest-based, etc.

In terms of politics, there is a good chance your party affiliation (or lack thereof) is based—at least in part—on your integration with whatever group you most identify with. Sometimes this is intentional (e.g., you're religious, and your spiritual beliefs compel you to vote a certain way), but often it is subconscious. Picture a lone conservative attending a school of the arts, where everyone around them—students and professors alike—lean left politically. While it is possible that the student would remain staunch in his beliefs, it is more likely that he would eventually begin to share many of their values and opinions, especially if he has high regard or respect for them.

We absorb. We adapt. Our clothing, behaviors, language, and beliefs become badges that signal our tribal affiliation.

If there is any vestige in your thoughts that we first *create* our belief systems and *then* seek out a "tribe" that shares them, it's time to abandon that notion. It's a more complicated dance of our unique psychological dispositions and life experiences, combined with other influences, that creates a dynamic feedback loop emphasizing tribal acceptance.

* * *

Virtue Signaling is "Tribal" Signaling

When it comes to interpersonal and intergroup relationships, I've become a tribalism *"primist"*—meaning that I see our need to belong to a group, and for that group to gain status and power, as the best lens for understanding our behavior. Much of what we do, say, and believe is instinctively concocted to help us gain acceptance by, and ensure belonging with, our chosen tribe. In his book, *Atomic Habits*, author James Clear explains, "Humans are herd animals. We want to fit in, bond with others, and earn the respect and approval of our peers. Such inclinations are essential to our survival. For most of our evolutionary history, our ancestors lived in tribes. Becoming separated from the tribe—or worse, being cast out—was a death sentence."[5a]

You want to please society. You want to be happy. You want to be well liked. You want to be held in high esteem and be respected...All of this requires conformity in some form or another.

THOMAS JANE

In 2004, the term *virtue signaling* entered the lexicon—a pejorative term for when one expresses a fake or insincere viewpoint with the intent of communicating good character or for the purpose of inclusion within a given group. More than merely grandstanding or putting on airs, *virtue-signaling* represents an individual's primal desire to gain or maintain the acceptance of their "tribe." And while the sentiment might be fabricated, the feelings can be very real. Research by psychologists Jillian Jordan and David Rand shows that "...even when people are unobserved—and thus have no incentive to signal their virtue—their sense of moral outrage is influenced by their desire to be seen positively by others."[5b] Further proof that our primitive brains are extremely complex, and the need for inclusion is foundational.

Virtue signaling might not be as inherently bad or counterfeit as one first believes. In my mind, all opinions, beliefs, and behaviors demonstrated in the public sphere are sincere even when adopted to prove conformity with a particular group. As Jordan points out, it could be that "you wouldn't have posted if there weren't reputational incentives to do so, but yet you genuinely feel outraged and you're not being inauthentic when you say that you care about the issue."[5c]

My quest to understand human behavior has included hundreds of personal interviews in which I've questioned why people believe what they believe and do what they do—especially about seemingly irrational and self-sabotaging behaviors. While their answers varied, one thing remained the same in *every* conversation—I *never* noted an *iota* of insincerity. When I attempted to challenge behaviors that I saw as being delusional or illogical, I was met with fierce resistance. (Interestingly, linguist David Shariatmadari argued in *The Guardian* that the very act of accusing someone of virtue signaling is an act of virtue signaling in and of itself.)[5d]

Because our primitive programming tells us that our best chance for survival is belonging to a tribe, we'll do whatever is necessary to ensure acceptance. What you see as delusion in others may in fact be a survival instinct at work. While discussing his book, *Useful Delusions*, NPR reporter Shankar Vendantam noted, "Many of us are often so upset with the content of people's delusions that we don't stop to ask the question: What is this delusion serving? What purpose? What psychological function is it serving?"[5e] *Brains are survival computers, not truth detectors—if self-deception will guarantee inclusion, the brain lies.* Facts don't matter. Morality doesn't matter. The only thing that matters is displaying the same tribal identifiers to avoid exclusion, because in your ancient brain *expulsion = death.*

* * *

My Way or The Highway

Because the constructs of our modern-day "tribes" are so varied (familial, religious, geographical, etc.), at times they may overlap. For example, "Jessica" is part of a geographical community (her progressive small town), but also part of an interest-based community (gun enthusiasts). If certain beliefs or values between her two "tribes" are at odds, this will create tension.

Picture the agnostic, liberal poet having dinner with his ultra-conservative, devoutly Christian mother. They may be part of the same family group, but their other allegiances are in conflict. It's not difficult to imagine that any discussion of politics could quickly escalate into a full-blown argument.

But *why?* Why do we argue so passionately about politics but not (usually) about everyday topics such as television, travel, traffic, or weather? Because politics has transcended being merely one of many values or beliefs held amongst "tribe" members. *Politics has become a "tribe" in and of itself.* And, as such, there is an ancient instinct in our brain to *protect the tribe* at all costs.

Luckily, we're (relatively) civilized, so these impulses don't immediately trigger physical violence as they might have in our ancient past. But the instincts—the literal *chemical* signals—are still there. Our limbic system is firing off a *fight or flight* response like an overheated nuclear reactor, while our prefrontal cortex (responsible for reason and executive function) is conflicted, trying to simultaneously do battle and remain calm.

No wonder we are so stressed and exhausted all the time! Our ancient brains weren't prepared to live in an interconnected society of varying beliefs and values. *"My way or the highway"*— we were programmed to be that stubborn.

* * *

The Politics of Fear: Your Triggers as Tools

As I mentioned previously, our tribal instincts leave us vulnerable, open to manipulation by those who would exploit our impulses for their own gain. Historically, one of the most effective forms of this exploitation has been creating a perceived "us vs. them" scenario. For example:

- *Adolf Hitler: By concocting a fictional narrative that the Jewish people (and others) were undermining the country, Hitler managed to turn many Germans against them. This ruthless propaganda campaign led to the deaths of millions.*
- *Joseph McCarthy: The one-term Senator from Wisconsin made his mark on American history by leading a crusade against communism. He played on Americans' fear of the Soviet Union to turn citizens against one another, making baseless accusations of treason and subversion, and leading*

a communist "witch hunt" that decimated careers, destroyed reputations, and cost millions.

Two of your most precious assets are your time and your attention . . . and, unfortunately, many groups know just how to push your buttons to gain control of both. Political parties, producers, corporations, politicians—they're all locked in a war, spending *trillions* of dollars annually to battle for your attention. In (extremely) broad terms, they have two options:

- *Fact-driven, slow-moving narratives that build human connections by way of empathetic understanding.*
- *Sensationalized, fast-paced, fear-driven messaging that triggers tribal reflexes and promotes division.*

One is expensive and time-consuming, the other quick and lucrative. Triggering ancient impulses not only grabs your attention but also changes your behavior—in particular, your *buying* behavior. **If they can get you to** *believe*, **they can get you to** *buy*—**be it product, premise, or promise.**

Make no mistake, *you're being played.* And yes, they absolutely know it. Now I'm not suggesting that all instances of tribalistic triggering come from an "evil" place— far from it. But we are being manipulated, and usually those

The propagandist's purpose is to make one set of people forget that certain other sets of people are human.

ALDOUS HUXLEY

responsible give little or no thought to what the long-term consequences of that might be, *or they just don't care.*

Remember: logic is slow, fear is fast.

Wait. Am I really implying that you're being intentionally frightened just to sell more advertising? That people are deliberately dividing America and upending our politics just to make a dollar?

Yes. That is *exactly* what I'm saying. And it's high time we stop playing into their hands and take back our lives.

* * *

Our Leaky Logic: What We Can't Unsee

If two identical people were to give you advice, in whom would you place more trust? It would depend on the topic, right? Sadly, not as much as you might think.

Epistemic Spillover is a phenomenon in which our doubt of or confidence in a person's knowledge in one area can "spill" into other, often unrelated, areas.

Picture this—you're in South America on vacation, and you're lost. You walk around asking if anyone speaks English. You receive conflicting directions from two pleasant and similar-looking people. The only major difference between them, aside from their differing navigational advice, is that one spoke in a British accent, the other in a standard American dialect. You've got to make a choice. Whose advice would you follow?

If your unthinking reaction is to follow the advice of the Brit, you're certainly not alone. Americans tend to add intelligence points to folks with British dialects. But how does that apply to the "lost in another country" scenario? Even if that British-speaking advice-giver *was* a bit smarter, that fact alone has no bearing on how familiar they are with this foreign city.

The above is an (admittedly over-simplified) example of epistemic spillover. We make certain assumptions about a person based on what we already know about them, and how we relate to what we know. In the case of politics, Americans tend to judge one another based on party labels, be that Republican, Democrat, Libertarian, Green, Socialist, Communist, or otherwise. But whether that raises or lowers our opinion of them depends on our *own* political affiliation.

For the sake of clarity, let's pretend there are only two political parties in the United States. And for the sake of neutrality, let's say they are the "Yellow Party" and the "Purple Party." If you are a tried-and-true Purple, and you believe the Purple Party's policies are right and just, and you believe the Yellow Party's policies will destroy the country, and everyone you trust is also faithfully Purple, there is an extraordinarily strong chance that when you run into a Yellow you will make snap (negative) judgments about their moral values, personality, and intelligence.

Americans seem to have an increasingly challenging time uncoupling what we know about a person politically from what we know about them personally.

How one voted wasn't always considered so integral to who we are, or how we perceive others, but these days we assign a tremendous amount of power to political affiliations (and their implied moral code). Think about it—that "party label" is often front-and-center on online dating profiles. Why? Because we believe it identifies us to others in a meaningful way and quickly shares a large amount of information about who we are. It's a badge we wear and, for many, someone donning a different badge would be an immediate "deal-breaker."

I once had a friend tell me that she had broken up with the man she was dating because she learned that he was, well, let's say a member of the Purple Party. She (a nonchalant Yellow) had been seeing him for a few months, and everything had been going quite well up to this point, so I asked her what had changed. She looked at me blankly and said, "*I just told you.*"

Can we really boil everything down to party affiliation? Is that sensible? Of course not. And yet, otherwise intelligent and well-meaning adults will dismantle friendships— some they've nurtured since childhood—based

The most damaging forms of intolerance are connected with religious, racial and political differences of opinion.

NAPOLEON HILL

on political stances or party affiliation. *We disagree on the minimum wage debate? We're breaking up. You've got a different opinion about immigration reform? It's over.*

Yet somehow we use these lost connections as fuel for our fire, convincing ourselves that these friendships failed because of the other person's poor moral code, mirrored in their selected political party.

Have we lost the ability to separate political views from personal identity?

Let us look at "Jesse" and "Joe." They were both raised in Tulsa and moved to Southern California. They both have a fantastic, dry sense of humor and hold the same religious beliefs. Both love travel, cooking, bluegrass music, Stephen King, the Star Wars franchise, and single malt scotch. But Joe is a gun enthusiast dedicated to protecting the second amendment, and Jesse passionately believes in gun law reforms. Should they dismiss the idea of a friendship based on that alone? What about all that they have in common?

We are complicated beings—heavily nuanced with moral values that have been influenced by time, age, upbringing, trauma, experiences, and more. You cannot sum up who a person is with their political affiliation. It's just not possible. And "scoring" a person's morality based on a party they have chosen, as opposed to the good or bad deeds they have done, is dangerous.

And yet, Americans continue to project onto those of different political parties everything taught by our own (chosen) political party, resulting in our thinking of them as literally "other."

The psychological and physiological ramifications of this "othering" behavior are alarming. Those who think of us as "other" may attempt to distance themselves or "shun" us, leaving us lonely and isolated. When humans are isolated, our confidence suffers, and we may experience feelings of betrayal, fear, depression, and anger.

But those who do the shunning suffer as well. By eschewing those with different political beliefs, we create a sort of "echo chamber"—an epistemic "bubble" shielding us from alternate views and current information. While this can feel quite comfortable and reassuring, in truth it is very damaging. It not only leaves us stagnant and unable to grow, but we may also begin to believe that we, and our opinions, are all there is. That everyone thinks as we do. That we are infallible. Our trust in those we surround ourselves with us expands, while our mistrust of "outsiders" intensifies.

We are good. They are evil.

You can see where this is going. Our epistemic spillover warps our perception of one another and creates debilitating division.

* * *

Tribalism is My Default Setting

From what I have observed and discovered in my own thinking, **intolerance is my default setting.** I have had to admit to myself that my mind is naturally distrusting of other people, and stereotypes them into different groups by any number of factors or characteristics, including but not limited to race, gender, religion, age, sexual orientation, nationality, profession, level of education, etc.

If you are thinking, "That's not me, I'm not intolerant," answer the following: Are you judgmental? Have you ever walked into a party filled with strangers and evaluated other people in the room, deciding who might be worth talking to and who wouldn't be? It might be common to call that behavior judgmental, but the truth is—that is a form of intolerance.

Our minds are quick to create divisions between ourselves and others, which can lead to inequities in privileges or discrimination.

- **Privileges:** Special advantages which are greater than the norm. *On a personal level, I might smile more broadly at, be more prone to engage in conversation with, or be more likely to do a favor for someone depending on the "group" I perceive them to be a part of. I'm not proud of it, and I don't try to do it (quite the opposite), but . . . there it is. On a societal level, an example might be granting employment opportunities based on stereotypes, or looking the other way at minor legal transgressions.*

- **Discrimination:** Withholding a right or privilege from one person or group that you would freely give to another. *Discrimination is sometimes very subtle and could be as simple as not "liking" someone's post on social media or smiling at everyone in a crowded room except a certain person or group of people. On a societal level, an example might be withholding access to school activities, scholarships, and sports, or denying employment opportunities, based on stereotypes.*

Because I am aware that my mind defaults to tribalism, I've tried to create a pattern of equity in my dealings with others, and I'd encourage you to do the same.

But while you are aware of a few specific areas in need of improvement, bear in mind that not all of our judgments are conscious. Sometimes we stereotype others, or have certain attitudes toward them, without being cognizant of it. Because I know that I might not be aware of all my implicit biases at any given moment, I've made an intentional effort to treat *everyone* I encounter with more than the ordinary amount of kindness, patience, and generosity. I *over*correct to thwart my primal tribalistic instincts and conquer my implicit biases. I'm certainly not perfect, and I'm certain I fall short at

> *I can tell if people are judgmental just by looking at them.*
>
> UNKNOWN

times, but in this type of endeavor, *any* improvement is worth making.

It's impossible to avoid all our ancient instincts and impulses. **But if our default is tribalism, what if we simply enlarged our tribes?**

Because I am dedicated to the well-being of our civilization, and the survival of our species, I've deliberately, purposefully expanded my "tribe" to the United States of America and humanity at large. The broader our "tribes" are, the less likely we are to end up in an epistemic bubble, and the better off everyone will be.

CHAPTER SIX

WHY DO WE ARGUE ABOUT POLITICS?

"Discussion is an exchange of knowledge; an argument an exchange of ignorance."

ROBERT QUILLEN

American Journalist, Humorist

P icture it: It's ten thousand years ago, and you and I are proud "Blue Facers." We decide to take a stroll through the forest. We arm ourselves with spears, paint our faces blue, and set out for a leisurely stroll.

As we turn a corner, we nearly collide with several "Green Facers"—their painted green faces an unmistakable "badge" signaling that they are *not* one of us. All of us—Blue and Green Facers alike—immediately take defensive postures, raise our spears, and begin yelling in our native tongues. Internally, our minds are being flooded with powerful hormones such as cortisol, adrenaline, and testosterone, driving us toward the highest levels of "fight or flight" mode. Maybe we battle, or maybe we back away, but one thing is certain—they are *not* with us. They are not part of our tribe, and they cannot be trusted.

You may be reading this thinking, "How silly. Can't they all see that they're the same under that green and blue face paint? How primitive we once were. I'm so much more sophisticated." But . . . *are you sure?*

Fast forward. You're having lunch with a group of friends when a social or political news story is brought up. It starts calmly enough, but then someone shares an opposing view. They are not sharing detailed analysis (and neither are you), you're all *just repeating talking points that have been fed to you by the "news" you've been consuming.* Faces grow red, volumes increase, people start cutting each other off, and it's starting to get personal. Exasperated, you think *"I can't understand how any reasonable person would believe that!"*

You've just re-enacted the modern-day equivalent of the ancient forest encounter.

Political arguments are not about issue discovery or developing empathy for opposing views, but about determining whether someone is *with you* or *against you.* Those sorts of "conversations," social media posts, and jokes are nothing more than "badges" indicating your tribal affiliation. Someone will no more likely correct an erroneous tribal belief than you would disavow a relationship with your family.

Your modern-day "badge" isn't green or blue face paint, it's what you believe.

We are much more civilized today, in that we're less likely to immediately resort to violence, but our ~~instincts~~* *evolved psychological mechanisms* haven't evolved enough for us to realize that subtle policy differences don't make someone an "other."

Have you ever been traveling and met someone new? You manage to get beyond shallow personal details into deeper territory such as politics, religion, upbringing, childhood trauma, or worldview. You find you have much in common, and before you know it, you're sharing your deepest secrets and vulnerable laughs.

You may believe you've met a "soul mate" of sorts, but it's just your tribalism identifying another member of your tribe. Of the 7.8 billion people on the planet, there are tens or hundreds of millions of others who share enough similar belief "badges" or life events to qualify—if you take enough time to get to know them.

---

* *I'm the oldest of five boys, and one of my brothers is an esteemed professor and researcher in Social Psychology. He was kind enough to have some conversations with me about this book early on. I was "trial ballooning" a concept and repeatedly used the word "instinct," resulting in this coarse interruption, "Stop saying that. They're not instincts, they're evolved psychological mechanisms." My brother is right; an evolved psychological mechanism is a psychological adaptation that a species takes on because of evolutionary pressures. Because an evolved psychological mechanism develops due to a survival need or adaptation, it typically helps the organism survive and reproduce, which encourages its transmission.*

Our evolved psychological mechanisms work the other way, too. When someone speaks in opposition to a core belief, it feels like an attack by an "other"—and our impulse to protect the "tribe" is sparked. We may also experience an acute sense of betrayal, especially when the opposition comes from friends or family, and that feeling only serves to bolster our defensiveness. Discussions quickly skip past the *conversational* to become *confrontational.* No longer about expanding knowledge, understanding, or empathy, they become nothing more than a struggle to "win."

Tribalism is the most powerful force in the world.

PATRICK DIXON

This is especially true of political conversations, which are becoming harder to side-step given that so many now wear their party preferences like symbolic badges signaling tribal affiliation. Sometimes this is in a figurative sense, but lately, and increasingly, it is literal. These outward displays act as a criterion, bluntly and directly asking others *"Are you with me or against me?"*

And *that* . . . that is the problem. The idea that one's political opinion alone could indicate whether they are friend or foe.

This is part of what motivates us to engage in arguments—because we cannot bear the thought of a friend or family member being on "the other side." To avoid losing them, we feel we must bring them into the fold of our "tribe," so we argue (fight) to *make* them understand.

The reality is—*arguing is futile.*

Honestly, we all know this. So why do we continue to do it?

Do you know someone who just *has* to be right all of the time? The truth is, this need is part of our ancient programming, and while we all feel it occasionally, it is due to our need to have confidence in the face of fighting that ancient "Green Facer" in the woods.

Our ancestor who didn't back down in the face of battle survived and was able to spread that genetic trait to their kin. In our primitive brains, we think of fighting to be "right," a form of "defending our territory." We also live in a highly competitive society, in which "winners" are rewarded and "losing" often carries undesirable consequences.

You can tell if someone is about social intercourse or just about browbeating somebody with their opinion. It's no fun arguing with a closed-minded person.

JOHN SCHNEIDER

One of the key problems with someone arguing to be *right* is that the other party must be *wrong*. You can see the trouble here. Even those who might be tolerant of an alternative point of view are apt to be extremely defensive when it is implied that their own views are "wrong."

When you create a win/lose scenario, no one is actively listening. No one is learning, and there is no understanding. It's just an argument—a useless game of tug-of-war.

* * *

Easier Said Than Done

Everyone has, at some point, looked back on an argument with regret. We think of what we should have said, what we should not have said, how we could have behaved better, or how we might have avoided the argument altogether. We might ask ourselves "Why did I get so worked up about that?"

How we *think* we must react in the moment and how we later realize we *should* have responded are two vastly different things, and, once again, we have evolutionary mismatching to thank for that. When we look back on intense arguments in a calm, cool, and collected manner it isn't because we no longer care about the subject matter: we are simply no longer in *survival* mode.

Think back to Saturday morning cartoons: when characters became agitated their faces would turn red, and steam would shoot out of their ears. These visuals were not invented out of thin air—they're exaggerated representations of what humans experience when their ancient brains perceive a threat. Emotions run high, of course, but real, physical changes take place as well. We may experience an increase in our heart rate, blood pressure, and temperature. We may stammer, sweat, or shake. Our body becomes physically stressed as our fight-or-flight response is triggered.

In this state, we aren't always making our best decisions. That is why—even if we've prepared ourselves for an interaction, even if we realize ahead of time that it could get out of hand, and even if we make a deliberate plan to remain calm—we can end up making regrettable choices. We may have intended to be a gracious host, but if we feel threatened, our instinct to attack may take over. We endeavor to dismantle the other party's argument as a way of depleting their "ammunition," and we strike first to avoid being struck. This isn't because we are hurtful, unintelligent, unfeeling, or melodramatic—we're simply attempting to protect ourselves from a perceived threat.

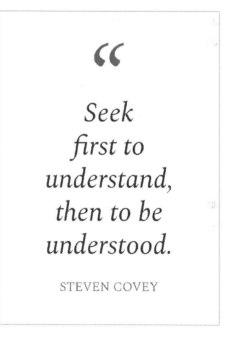

Seek first to understand, then to be understood.

STEVEN COVEY

We want to be right, but we also want to feel safe, understood, and accepted. When our beliefs are questioned, ridiculed, or attacked—or if we *perceive* that this is happening—our defenses are triggered.

The majority of people cannot differentiate *who they are* from *what they believe*. Most think they are what they believe. Early on, I was challenged to make a solid distinction that *I am not what I believe*. It was one of the most important decisions I have ever made in my life, allowing me to be less defensive and 100% willing to drop a false belief for truth.

> *I have no loyalty to my beliefs – all of my beliefs are temporary pending new information.*

Beyond our need to be right is our need to be understood, and accepted. When a person questions our beliefs or ridicules them, we project that condemnation back onto ourselves. We take the feedback personally and believe the person is critical of us rather than a belief we hold. Feeling this way, we become defensive, prepared to keep fighting until we "win" the argument.

Understanding what triggers our own "attack mode" is a crucial first step toward mastering the art of conversation. It isn't easy, and we shouldn't beat ourselves up when we fall short. (Read that last line again.) That said, we should always strive to do better. To maintain and grow our relationships, we must approach conversations with respect and acceptance, learn to overcome competitive thinking, and strive to seek out common ground.

CHAPTER SEVEN

THE DEATH OF TOLERANCE

"Tolerance has never been the cause of civil war; while, on the contrary, persecution has covered the earth with blood and carnage."

VOLTAIRE

17th Century French Writer, Historian, Philosopher

H ave you ever had a conversation with a trusted friend in which you vented your frustrations about the annoying actions or behavior of a co-worker, family member, boss, or mutual acquaintance? Perhaps your friend nodded in agreement, and the two of you wondered what would possess a person to act that way. You may have even joked about how much better the world would be if everyone thought like, and were as wonderful as, the two of you.

If you have, don't be too hard on yourself. Even the kindest people I know have had interactions like these. Some behaviors are incredibly difficult to deal with—especially if they're quite different from your own and you don't fully understand them.

While it doesn't make you a bad person, it means you are being *intolerant*. The oft-misunderstood concept of *inclusion* does not mean that you must agree with or adopt thoughts, behaviors, actions, or ideas that you disagree with or dislike. Rather, it means allowing them. Allowing them to exist, alongside your own thoughts, behaviors, actions, or ideas, and recognizing that they have a right to exist (provided they are legal, they don't hurt others, etc.).

Want to be happy? Be more inclusive. While some may debate whether happy people are more inclusive, or inclusive people are happier, research has shown that the two go hand-in-hand.[7a]

But what should be tolerated, what should not, and how do we tell the difference?

* * *

Tolerance of Actions and Activities

Broadly speaking, if it doesn't hurt or hinder, and it's legal, it should probably be tolerated. Our country was founded on freedom and liberty, and our founders guaranteed the following in our Bill of Rights:

- **The right to free speech.** *The First Amendment guarantees the right to freedom of speech, freedom of the press, and freedom to assemble peaceably.*

- **The right to bear arms.** *The Second Amendment guarantees each state's right to keep a militia, and (arguably) the right of individuals to keep firearms.*

- **No unauthorized quartering of soldiers.** *The Third Amendment prohibits soldiers from being quartered in private residences during peacetime without permission, or during war time except under special circumstances.*

- **Freedom from search and seizure.** *The Fourth Amendment guarantees the right against search and seizure of personal property or private papers.*

- **Freedom from self-incrimination.** *The Fifth Amendment protects against self-incrimination and double jeopardy, and guarantees due process.*

- **Trial by jury.** *Under the Sixth Amendment, individuals have a right to be tried by a jury of their peers in criminal cases. The Seventh Amendment guarantees trial by jury in civil cases involving certain set sums of money.*

On the other hand, for reasons that are core to both our nature and our enculturation, all forms of the following are seen as being intolerable (apart from very narrowly defined acts of protection):

- **Violence**
- **Destruction of property**
- **Assault** (the physical threat of violence)
- **Intimidation** (the threat of injury to a person, reputation, or property with intent to cause harm)
- **Reckless endangerment** (the creation of a substantial risk of serious physical injury to another person)

In the past two centuries, through local, state, and federal law, our government has been given a monopoly on violence. As noted by neuroscientist and philosopher Sam Harris, *"Giving a monopoly on violence to the state is just about the best thing we have ever done as a species. It ranks right up there with keeping our fecal matter out of our food. Having a police force that can deter crime, and solve crimes when they occur, and deliver violent criminals to a functioning justice system is the necessary precondition for almost anything else of value in society.*"[7b]

But, at times, law enforcement or the federal government may exceed their limitations about violence, or abuse their power. When they do, they must be held to account. However, this does not suddenly permit us to carry out the acts mentioned above. *Legally*, there is *no* permissible reason for taking up arms against the government. This includes:

- *When we disagree with laws*
- *When we disagree with actions of government officials*
- *When we disagree with actions of government agencies*
- *When we disagree with the outcome of an election*

The only reasons it might be justifiable (though still not legal) to take up arms against our government would be speculative and difficult to imagine. If I were to attempt to envision these scenarios, they might include such extreme circumstances as:

- *Nationwide revocation of all individual protections afforded citizens in the Constitution*
- *Elimination of all judicial processes at the national, state, and local levels*
- *Nationwide elimination of the right to petition the government for a redress of grievances*
- *Widespread jailing of citizens, combined with the elimination of due process*

* * *

Tolerance of Ideas

There is no shortage of ideas. We have them. Others have them. They're shared broadly, every day, on screens, pages, and from pulpits. Some are good, some aren't so good, some are verifiably bad and belong in the scrapheap of history (asbestos, Agent Orange, New Coke).

But seriously, what if a friend raised an idea you considered outlandish, in poor taste, or downright reprehensible?

First, it's important to understand that we are not our thoughts. This concept can be tricky because many people think they are what they believe—that their thoughts are who they are, and the two cannot be separated. Knowing what I know about neuroscience and philosophy, I don't believe this to be true. Thoughts are incredibly transient, malleable, and subjective. (Consider this: there must have been thoughts that you held sacred just ten years ago that you have since completely abandoned.)

When friends of mine raise ideas that I find to be bizarre or simply wrong, I'm careful to listen to them. I do my best to see things from their point of view. Only after I feel I have fully absorbed the idea, and the reasons behind it, do I (civilly) offer rebuttal—if necessary.

Freedom of speech (and, by extension, ideas) is one of our most sacred rights from a legal standpoint, and all ideas should be tolerated. However, there are some expressions of ideas that we have determined to be *intolerable (illegal or open to regulation)*; these include (but are not limited to): [7c]

- Incitement of violence, riots, etc.
- Threats of violence

- Obscenity
- Child pornography
- Threatening the President of the United States

* * *

Tolerance of Objects

Very generally speaking, if an object is not doing (and does not have the potential to do) harm, it should be tolerated.

While a particular sculpture might offend you, that does not override the right of the artist to create or display it. However, there are gray areas and exceptions. If the artist were to mount the sculpture in a way that obstructed the view of drivers, creating the potential for accidents that could result in injury or death, the *position* of the object would certainly be intolerable (but not the object itself). If the object were made of a material that, when looked upon, caused irreparable damage to the human eye, then certainly the object itself would be considered intolerable.

Our governing bodies have made some objects illegal or placed heavy regulations upon them. This is due to safety concerns and applies when something possesses the ability to harm humans or the environment severely or permanently. This includes (but is not limited to):

- Weapons
- Waste
- Chemicals
- Industrial and manufacturing plants
- Heavy machinery
- Aerospace vehicles

***

Tolerance of People
(This Must End)

Yes, you read that right. I reject the use of the word "tolerance" about human beings. In terms of how we relate to others, *tolerance* is just a slightly milder form of *intolerance*.

Two things are at the heart of "tolerating" others:

1) **Distinction:** *A declaration of difference between you—that they are somehow "other."*

2) **Arrogance:** *The intrinsic conviction that you or your ideas are in some way superior. (You've determined that it is you who must do the tolerating, not the other way around.)*

Philosopher Jiddu Krishnamurti explains this beautifully, noting, "The tolerance of which you speak is merely a clever invention of the mind; this tolerance merely indicates the desire to cling to your own idiosyncrasies, your own limited ideas and prejudices, and allow another to pursue his own. In this tolerance, there is no intelligent diversity, but only a kind of superior indifference. There is utter falsity in this tolerance. You say, 'You continue in your own way, and I shall continue in mine; but let us be tolerant, brotherly.' When there is true brotherliness, friendliness, when there is love in your heart, then you will not talk of tolerance. Only when you feel superior in your certainty, in your position, in your knowledge, only then do you talk of tolerance."[7d]

As a society, our goal should be to transcend mere toleration in favor of genuine *inclusion*.

Humans need to belong. We crave it. We have a fundamental yearning to feel that we are an integral part of something *more*. In fact, "belongingness" is at the center of Maslow's famous Hierarchy of Needs, positioned just above our need for safety.[7e]

Maslow's Hierarchy of Needs

Self Actualization

Esteem Needs

Belongingness and Love

Safety Needs

Physiological Needs

It is important, however, to realize that simply "fitting in" is not enough. As esteemed researcher Brené Brown explains, "Fitting in is about assessing a situation and becoming who you need to be to be accepted. Belonging, on the other hand, doesn't require us to change who we are; it requires us to be who we are."[7f]

In simple terms, here is how I see it:

- Intolerance: *You're not like us, and we reject you.*
- Tolerance: *You're not like us, we're better than you, but we'll put up with you.*

- Fitting in: *You're trying to be like us, and that's ok.*
- Inclusion (genuine acceptance): *You are you; we wouldn't be the same without you, and you are essential.*

Toleration is only slightly better than *intolerance*. It's like a reduced-fat version of a decadent dessert—still bad for you.

* * *

The Benefits of Belonging

Does it feel good to exclude others? Does it benefit you in a positive and meaningful way? Of course not. So why do we do it? For some, it might have to do with a need to establish and solidify the identity of self or "tribe." To clarify what we *are*, we feel the need to reject what we *aren't*. But this is as unhelpful as it is unnecessary.

You might find the ideas, actions, behaviors, belief systems, or affiliations of others offensive, but the best pathway forward—both for yourself *and* for society at large—is to accept them into your "tribe." You can demonstrate their belonging in the following ways:

- **The equal provision of privileges.** *Evenly applying advantages or granting immunity, regardless of factors such as political orientation, race, religion, nationality, gender, sexual orientation, etc.*
    - *Advantages might include kindnesses and courtesies, such as smiles, conversations, favors, jobs, loans, recommendations, etc.*

o   *Immunity might include forgiving unpaid loans, not enforcing a boundary, excusing a minor intrusion, etc.*

- **The absence of discrimination.** *Discrimination is to withhold a privilege freely given to others. In the absence of discrimination, we do not withhold advantages or immunity based on "who" someone is (political orientation, race, religion, nationality, gender, sexual orientation, etc.).*

Human beings are incredibly anxious creatures, predisposed to feelings of alienation and unworthiness. When our sense of connection and acceptance is threatened, our ability to self-regulate and survive suffers, and we are prone to depression, anxiety, anti-social behavior, crime, racism, and violence. But when we truly feel we belong, we are healthier and happier. We experience feelings of safety and security, we are driven to form connections and to work toward shared goals, and we are better able to cope with stress.

On a societal level, there are innumerable potential benefits of "belongingness," including (but certainly not limited to):

- **Increased motivation**
- **Better cooperation**
- **Improved problem solving**
- **Reduced bullying**
- **Less crime**
- **Fewer mental health issues**
- **Improved health overall**
- **Longer lifespans**

Belonging is powerful. Happiness and well-being depend on it, so it is in our best interest to work toward creating *a society of belonging*—in which people feel both valued and accepted.

* * *

Are You a Bigot?

One of the worst smears is to be called a racist. A racist discriminates against others based on skin color, ethnicity, or nation of origin. Here is what racism frequently looks like:

- **Internal Distinctions**
  An individual makes an internal distinction that someone else is an "other" or "not like me." This may be done consciously or subconsciously, as quickly as in the blink of an eye.

- **Stereotyping**
  Our brains are quite adept at recognizing and creating patterns (often where they don't exist), and we begin by identifying what we see as being the distinctions between "us" and "them." These stereotypes and generalizations lead us down a dangerous path of non-inclusion.

- **External Expression**
  We begin to communicate these differences with others on "our" side, to determine if they've noticed the same things that we have. Are we justified in making them "others"?

- **Disassociation**
  We unfriend or distance ourselves from the "others," or expel them from our social group.

- **Dehumanization and Slurs**
  If our findings are reinforced by individual experiences, agreement from within our community, or stories in the media—and if we believe that we might be in competition with the "others"—we begin to dehumanize them. Using stereotypes as a foundation, we create derogatory, cruel labels to diminish and demean the "others." All slurs are marked indications of intolerance.

> *Bigotry and judgment are the height of insecurity.*
>
> JASMINE GUY

- **Discrimination**
  We withdraw a privilege—something we would give freely to everyone else. This could be as seemingly small as withholding eye contact, grins, waves, and kind gestures (such as opening doors), or it could be worse—we might deny them courteousness in an overt manner to ensure they are aware of the discrimination, (such as looking someone in the eye as we

close a door in their face). Other forms of discrimination could include not interviewing, hiring, or granting raises to the "others," or denying them housing, service, etc.

- **Violence**
  With enough support from "our" group, we might even feel that violence is not only needed but also justified. We might look for ways to violently intimidate, abuse, or remove the "others."

Reading the above, you might be horrified, and you might be thinking "I would never do these things, and I'd quickly disassociate with anyone who did." But the above behaviors aren't exclusive to racism.

big·ot
/ˈbigət/
noun

A person who is intolerant of and biased against dissimilar *creeds*, *beliefs*, or *opinions*.

Someone who is irrationally, inflexibly connected to a conviction, judgment, or faction; in particular, antagonism and/or prejudice against others based on their belonging to a particular group.

Many people erroneously believe that the definition of "bigot" is "a racist." As you can see, it is more encompassing than that. Facing our own intolerance can be difficult, but the work is important. To that end, I will ask that you review the following questions and answer them as honestly as possible:

1. Have you ever, even only in your mind, labeled someone else any of the following: *Blowhard, Elitist, Extremist, Fanatic, Fool, Fringe, Hack, Hippie, Hypocrite, Ideologue,*

Idiot, Jackass, Lemming, Loser, Misogynist, Moron, Nutjob, Obstructionist, Racist, Scum, Shill, Thug, Trash, Troll, Twit, Wacko, or Zealot?

2. Have you ever referred to someone on the left of the ideological spectrum as: *Bleeding Heart, Commie, Cupcake, Feminazi, Globalist, Lib, Liberocrat, Libtard, Obamination, Obamunist, Obama-zombie, PC (Politically Correct), Snowflake, Social Justice Warrior, Socialist?*

3. Have you ever referred to someone on the right of the ideological spectrum as: *Basement Dweller, Birther, Conspiratard, Deplorable, Drumpf-ster, Fascist, MAGA-Head, Red Hatter, Republicrite, Repugnican, Re-thug-lican, Teabagger, Teapublican, Trumpkin, Trumpster, Trumptard?*

4. Have you ever discriminated *(review description above)* against people of another political persuasion?

5. Have you ever disassociated with, defriended, or alienated someone (family, social media friend, or real-world friend) because of their political beliefs?

If you answered yes to any of the above, you've committed acts of bigotry. **It is time to end all bigotry in our country. Bigotry is bigotry.**

Intolerance is to stand alone.
Tolerance is to stumble separately.
Inclusion is to walk together.

CHAPTER EIGHT

TAKE
YOUR LIFE
BACK

"The lizard brain is hungry, scared, angry, and horny. The lizard brain only wants to eat and be safe. The lizard brain will fight (to the death) if it has to, but would rather run away. It likes a vendetta and has no trouble getting angry."

SETH GODIN

Author, Speaker, Entrepreneur

L izard brain, ancient brain . . . no matter what you chose to call it, our deeply coded programming can be problematic for us, at times, in the modern world. The good news is, we are capable of "outsmarting" it if we are willing to do a little work.

Below you will find what I like to call "*9 Realizations to Help You Take Back Your Life.*" I use the term "realizations" because these are things I have come to realize after making every mistake in this book at least a thousand times. They resulted from (or despite) more than thirty years of beating my head against the proverbial wall. Once you realize these and act accordingly, your life (and the lives of those around you) will undoubtedly change for the better.

* * *

REALIZATION ONE:

I am a towering mountain of ignorance.

When I began my business career, I was young, arrogant, and self-righteous. Now I'm middle-aged, humble, and ignorant.

To get from there to here took upwards of thirty years. During that time, I read books (about one per week), listened to over 2,500 hours (about 3 and a half months) of podcasts, and attended at least a week or more of personal or professional training each year. All this information and education has led me to one startling and significant conclusion:

I don't know much.

I am less certain of my own knowledge now than I have been at any other point in my life. The more I learn, the more I realize that what I know is so small, what *I know I do not know* is so vast, and *what I do not know I do not know* is *spectacularly breathtaking.*

* * *

REALIZATION TWO:

All of my knowledge is temporary pending new information.

Amateur philosopher Matt Dillahunty once said, "I want to believe as many true things and as few false things as possible."[8a] That advice seems so simple and so obvious, but *have you ever made that decision?* I have, and the effect has been profound. I no longer argue over information someone else believes to be true because I realize that what I believe may not be true. Instead, I use their informational challenge as an opportunity to fact-check myself. I hold on to the knowledge in my head lightly, and I continually look for opportunities to upgrade "bad" (outdated, inaccurate) information with "good" (current, accurate).

* * *

REALIZATION THREE:

It's easier to fool people than to convince them that they have been fooled.

This realization is often attributed to Mark Twain, and for most of my life that is who I believed had penned it. But as I mentioned, I am constantly looking for opportunities to update my information. In this case, I learned that Twain was not responsible for the hot take above. (The original author is *unknown.*) Regardless of who first said it, the concept holds up.

One would think that when our beliefs were challenged with facts, we would update our thinking accordingly. However, surprisingly, the opposite is often true. When counterevidence is presented, rather than accepting it and doubting or changing our views, our conviction in them grows stronger. We double-down on our beliefs in the face of factual evidence to the contrary. This is a cognitive bias known as the *Backfire Effect*.

"Faced with a choice between changing one's mind and proving there is no need to do so," wrote economist J.K. Galbraith, "almost everyone gets busy with the proof."[8b]

If you want a friend to stop holding a belief that is untrue, *stop talking about it.* You may think that challenging their view repeatedly will eventually wear them down, but it could have the opposite effect.

Repetition is the fuel of falsehoods.

Those who would like us to believe a lie are very aware of this. Former Soviet Premier Vladimir Lenin once said, "A lie told often enough becomes the truth." Nazi chief propagandist Joseph Goebbels said it this way, "If you tell a lie big enough and keep repeating it, people will eventually come to believe it."

These statements remain as true today as they were a century ago. The constant din of 24-hour news networks creates a turbo-charged information tornado with the capacity to expose viewers to the same lie dozens or even hundreds of times per day. This rhythmic reiteration creates *illusory truth*. Repeated exposure increases the impression of truth, regardless of credibility—even in the case of something we previously *knew* was untrue!

Remember this when it comes to lies: Lies must be repeated to live.

* * *

REALIZATION FOUR:
The best way to change someone's mind is through relationships.

When someone holds a view that is the opposite of our own, it can be confusing, annoying, or even infuriating. Our instinct is often to "help" them by attempting to change their mind—by arguing our viewpoint until they "see the light." However, as noted above, this is ineffective, as *their* instinct is likely to grip their opinions even more tightly to protect their beliefs. Finally, out of frustration, we (or they) decide that distance (unfriending, blocking) is the only answer, and we part ways.

That is the worst thing you could do. We have already covered some of the reasons for this, but here's another—relationships change minds. If you cut off the relationship, you're cutting off your best chance of finding common ground.

When I met my amazing wife, we were politically divergent. Our worldviews were quite different, and disagreements were common. But although we debated and often locked horns early on, we never attempted to alter one another's viewpoints.

Over a period of about ten years, a remarkable thing happened: we transmuted to sharing *identical* worldviews. But *how?* Through thoughtful discussions; shared experiences; consumption of many of the same books, films, and podcasts; and thousands of hours of empathetic conversation. Most importantly, through it all, *we were not trying to change the other person's mind.*

When two parties both feel safe in their own beliefs, and secure in their relationship, they can explore different viewpoints without feeling a need to attack or defend. This is how new information is considered, weighed, and accepted. The example I gave is of a romantic relationship, but the same applies to familial relationships, friendships, etc.

Convincing someone to change their mind is really the process of persuading them to change their community affiliation ("tribe"). But if they abandon their beliefs, they run the risk of severing social ties, so this is no simple feat. Nobody wants their worldview torn apart, and if loneliness is the outcome it becomes even less appealing.

"People are embraced or condemned according to their beliefs," said Steven Pinker, Harvard psychologist, "so one function of the mind may be to hold beliefs that bring the belief-holder the greatest number of allies, protectors, or disciples, rather than beliefs that are most likely to be true."[8c]

If you genuinely want to change someone's mind, become friends with them. You cannot expect someone to alter their views if you take away their community, too, so you must give them somewhere to go. By bringing them into your circle and integrating them into your community, they can safely rethink their beliefs without fear of social abandonment.

It is not difference so much as distance that breeds tribalism—and, by extension, hostility. As proximity increases, so does understanding. I am reminded of Abraham Lincoln's quote: "I don't like that man. I must get to know him better."

Arguments do not change people's minds—relationships do.

***

REALIZATION FIVE:
Never argue with someone
on social media. Ever.

"Oh, wow, that post completely changed my beliefs," said absolutely no one. The three and a half minutes you spend posting a thoughtful quote, meme, link to a news article, or carefully worded refutation is not going to change someone's mind. I'm sorry, but there it is—it's just not going to happen.

You might say, "But I don't have thousands of hours and ten years to change this guy's opinion online." Exactly. If it takes two people in an intimate human relationship a decade to accept and adopt one another's beliefs, what makes you think a hasty argument on Facebook is going to change anyone's mind?

When you argue with someone online, here are some (but certainly not all) of the negative consequences:

- **You provoke.** *Calling someone out publicly is a bad idea, and I'm sure I don't need to explain why. All you're doing is activating their defensive instincts and embarrassing them in the process. This may cause them to dig their heels in deeper, and it could trigger a counterattack.*

- **You attract attention.** *Social media algorithms may promote your argument on more feeds, which only spreads divisiveness, anger, and misunderstanding beyond the original audience. More people will read the arguments and reinforce the views of either side without changing their own.*

- **You get in your own way.** *No matter how righteous or justified you feel, you very well could be wrong (or at least have misinformation). By arguing online, you only further entrench yourself in what might be an inaccurate belief. You create a hill that your pride can want you to die on. None of us are perfect. We've all been wrong before, and we're all certainly wrong about many things at this very moment. If you're not able to consider the possibility that you're wrong, you need to work on that.*

- **You exacerbate.** *The more you talk about—whatever it is—the more it embeds itself in someone's mind, and the more it spreads. Much like depriving a fire of wood will cause it to burn out, one of the best ways to extinguish a bad idea is to stop talking about it.*

When we see a post that is offensive, dissenting, or just plain false, the impulse to defend, disprove, or deny can be difficult to resist. But engaging in online debates is going to do more harm than good.

* * *

REALIZATION SIX:

The wise man knows his own mind
well enough to distrust it.

Our minds make hundreds, if not thousands, of snap decisions or assumptions every day using the (often imperfect) information we have at our disposal. Choices made so quickly and automatically that we might not even be consciously involved in the process. These systematic and frequently flawed responses are made with the assistance of *Cognitive Bias*—faulty patterns of thinking coded into our ancient brains. These biases are false distortions of reality that lead to bad decisions.

While there are thought to be 180 Cognitive Biases[8d], one of the biggest (at least in my estimation) is *confirmation bias*. We want to continue to believe what we already believe, so we seek out information that supports or validates our views, and we interpret data in a way that is "comfortable" for our current knowledge. If we're staunchly devoted to a political candidate, for example, we seek out opinion pieces and news articles that reaffirm our confidence in them.

Confirmation bias shows up most blatantly in our current political divide, where each side seems unable to allow that the other side is right about anything.

BEN YAGODA

When faced with nebulous information, we may process it in a way that favors our existing view.

But we don't simply pursue evidence that *supports* our current knowledge—we also tend to be dismissive of information that may *refute* a previously held belief. This is known as *disconfirmation bias*, and, as with confirmation bias, it is stronger when we are emotionally connected to, or strongly invested in, maintaining a particular opinion.

For example, if we thought the vase in our doctor's office was *blue*, and someone told us that it was *purple*, we wouldn't have any trouble accepting that information. We didn't care one way or another. Our belief about the color of the vase was not important to us, and changing that belief has no measurable impact. We accept the information without resistance or delay, and we move on.

On the other hand, if you have been staunchly devoted to a political candidate for many years and you're suddenly faced with information suggesting they are *not* as righteous or honest as you believe them to be, your disconfirmation bias is likely to kick in. It might compel you to reject that information—with little or no critical review—to avoid having to reassess your opinions.

The sad news is it would be impossible to completely eradicate these biases. The good news is that we can learn to reduce and manage them. Beyond simply attempting to look at information objectively, we must commit ourselves to being skeptical of our ideas and opinions. The more deeply rooted they are, the more important it is that we seek out and consider evidence to the contrary.

> ❝
>
> *If there's something you really want to believe, that's what you should question the most.*
>
> PENN JILLETTE

110

Bottom line: If we want to develop unbiased opinions and seek for truth, we must start by distrusting our own minds.

* * *

REALIZATION SEVEN:
My job is to discover where I'm wrong, not to make someone else wrong.

Years ago, when I first ventured onto social media, if I discovered someone had shared misinformation I would leap into action. *"Step back everyone—someone is wrong on the internet! I will handle this!"* I'd search cyberspace, find evidence to the contrary, and kindly reply with a link to the accurate information.

Strangely enough, no one was ever very appreciative.

Occasionally I would come across a negative meme or article about a politician I did not agree with, and I would instantly assume it was true—my cognitive biases in full effect. Once in a while, I would even share the post or article (sometimes without reading past the headline), only to have to retract it later when I learned it was fallacious.

What did I learn? **Fact check what you want to believe, not what you want to disprove.**

When we put the focus on being more accurate ourselves, rather than pointing out where others are wrong, we not only learn and grow in meaningful ways, but we also directly address the problem of propaganda. The best way to extinguish misinformation is to stop repeating it. Mind what you, yourself, are sharing and believing. Double-check your beliefs for accuracy, especially when it comes to things you desperately want to be true. Remember, trying to change someone else's mind is worthless, but changing *your own* mind is priceless.

* * *

REALIZATION EIGHT:
Arguing with your friends is not fighting for your country.

We all believe the political opinions we hold are correct and in the best interest of our country and fellow citizens. So when we hear someone promote an ideology, value, or political opinion that is in opposition to our own, it can trigger several ancient impulses within us.

But without a doubt, the reason many choose to argue politics is a feeling that they must stand up for and protect our country. No matter how you felt about those who stormed the Capitol on January 6th, one thing was clear—they were confident that they were fighting for their country. They were convinced of it.

When we believe our "tribe" to be in danger, our protective instincts erupt like a volcano, vaulting us into action. This does not apply only to physical or widespread threats. The beliefs and opinions of just one person can trigger our defensive impulses, and when the weapons of the perceived oppressor are words and ideas, we often fire back in kind.

We argue.

The rush of adrenaline and dopamine we experience may feel incredible, making us believe that we are righteous and effective. But that is an illusion. We are not doing anything meaningful or helpful when we argue. All we are doing is driving a wedge between ourselves and those we disagree with, and further entrenching ourselves in our insular bubble.

* * *

REALIZATION NINE:

The President of the United States doesn't matter as much as you think–or in the way that you think.

In the film *Meatballs*, Bill Murray memorably led a chant of "It just doesn't matter! It just doesn't matter!" At the time, I didn't really understand it. Now I do. Indulge me for a moment, and take the short quiz below....

1. **Which President below was *worst* for the country?**

   ____ George H.W. Bush *(1989 to 1993)*

   ____ Bill Clinton *(1993 to 2001)*

   ____ George W. Bush *(2001 to 2009)*

   ____ Barack Obama *(2009 to 2017)*

2. **On a scale of 0 to 10 (0 being best, 10 being worst), how bad were they for the country?**

   ____

3. What made them so terrible? List their worst
    decisions and policies.

_____

_____

4. Since their initial inauguration date, what have been
    the biggest changes in your life?

_____

_____

Now, compare your answers to questions 3 and 4. Are there any in common? *Probably not.* Now, of course, just because something does not impact *you* does not mean that it is not important. But the comparison is worth thinking about.

Looking back at our nation's history, if we weigh our level of fervor, emotion, and intensity about who will become President against the resulting presidencies, we will find that it has been grossly disproportionate. In the past, I have gotten myself fairly worked up, subconsciously believing something a little too close to "the world will end if this candidate wins" and "everything will be wonderful if that candidate wins."

In the end, *neither was true.*

As I am authoring this book, we have just completed one of the most anomalous presidencies in our nation's history, so I will not go as far as to say that a future President could not create an existential threat to our nation. As they say in the financial world, "Past performance is no guarantee of future results." While that may be true, there is much we can learn from studying our history.

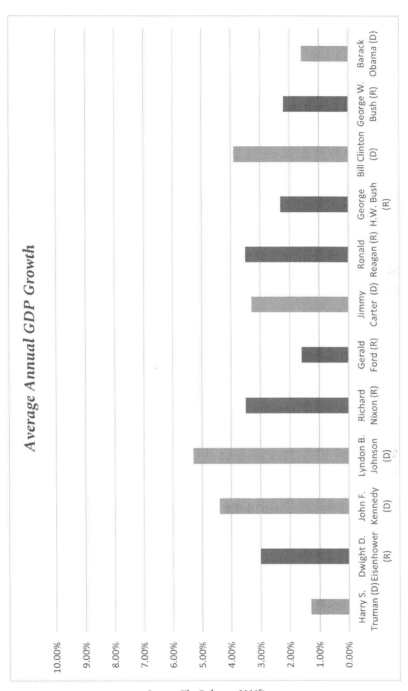

Average Annual GDP Growth

Harry S. Truman (D) · Dwight D. Eisenhower (R) · John F. Kennedy (D) · Lyndon B. Johnson (D) · Richard Nixon (R) · Gerald Ford (R) · Jimmy Carter (D) · Ronald Reagan (R) · George H.W. Bush (R) · Bill Clinton (D) · George W. Bush (R) · Barack Obama (D)

10.00% · 9.00% · 8.00% · 7.00% · 6.00% · 5.00% · 4.00% · 3.00% · 2.00% · 1.00% · 0.00%

Source: The Balance, 2020[8e]

115

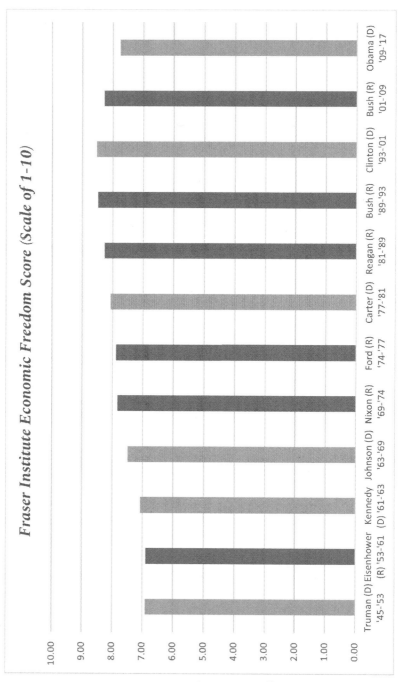

Fraser Institute Economic Freedom Score (Scale of 1-10)

Source: Our World in Data, 2018[8f]

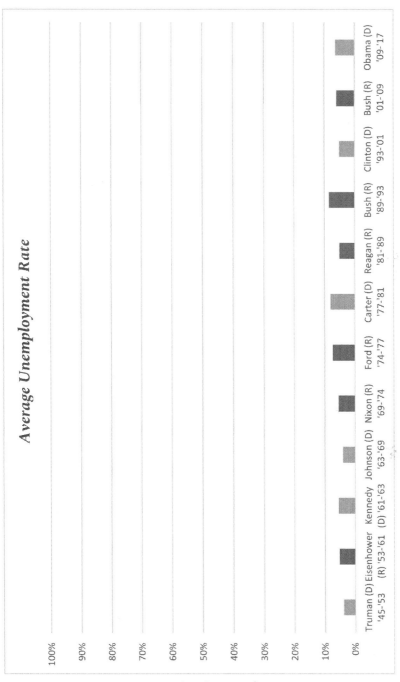

Average Unemployment Rate

Source: The Balance, 2019[8g]

There is a time-tested question utilized by several opinion polling services known as *Right Direction or Wrong Track*. It's usually asked via phone call, during which the pollster asks, "Do you believe the country is headed in the right or wrong direction?" The results are not that surprising, considering our tribalistic nature.

- A vast majority of *Republicans* believe the country is headed in the wrong direction *mere days* after a *Democrat* is inaugurated.

- A vast majority of *Democrats* believe the country is headed in the wrong direction *mere days* after a *Republican* is inaugurated.

According to most historians, it takes 2 to 3 years before a President's policies truly begin to change a country's trajectory. Our opinion about the state of the union, at any given time, is more often a reflection of our tribalism than reflective of the nation's actual current condition.

Our ancient instincts compel us to believe things about Presidents, parties, and policies that may not be true. Does the POTUS really impact our country to the degree we believe them to? Consider the following:

- **Stock market.** We often pin stock market performance on Presidents. But as professor and author Jeremy Siegel noted, "Bull markets and bear markets come and go, and it's more to do with business cycles than presidents." Barron's deputy editor, Ben Levisohn, seems to agree, stating bluntly, "The stock market doesn't care who the President is."[8h, 8i]

- **GDP growth.** This averages just under 3% per year and the sitting President has extraordinarily little impact on it. *New York Times* senior economics correspondent, Neil Irwin, explained, "Presidential reputations rise or fall with gross domestic product. [...] But the reality is that presidents have far less control over the economy than you might imagine."[8j, 8k]

- **Unemployment.** If you lose or gain a job it is more due to macroeconomic trends or your personal performance rather than a President's actions. Noah Smith of the *Chicago Tribune* opined, "I always laugh when I see stories asking how many jobs the president has created. [...] Even if presidents' policies do manage to help the economy, it's hard to quantify their impact."[8l]

Let me be abundantly clear: Presidents matter. Voting matters. As citizens of the United States, it is our responsibility to participate in the democratic process, and we *should* care who is elected, and it *does* matter. **My point is only that our opinions about these decisions don't warrant the alarmingly high level of conflict and division we've reached. You could still effectively vote in the next election and financially contribute to the party or the candidate of your choice while reducing the time and attention you devote to politics by 99%.**

News, Media, and Personalities:
Fear the Fearmonger

"The thing you fear most has no power.
Your fear of it is what has the power."

OPRAH WINFREY
American Author, Philanthropist, Talk Show Personality

CHAPTER NINE

ARE YOU ADDICTED TO FEAR?

*"The only thing we have to fear
is fear itself."*

FRANKLIN D. ROOSEVELT

32nd President of the United States of America

What is your relationship with the news? Do you love it? Hate it? How much of it do you consume? How much of that is germane or necessary?

The first 24-hour television news network debuted in June of 1980. At the time, I remember hearing many people ask "How on earth will they find enough news to stay on all day?" It seemed like a fair question. Prior to its launch, most of us got our news from a daily paper, in five minute radio bursts on our drive to work, or by way of nightly, hour-long television broadcasts—and we felt well informed by that. So how was this new network going to fill so many hours, every day? And, more importantly, what would be the benefit?

We soon realized that two of the biggest benefits were being able to view television news on our own schedule and being able to see news as it happened. Previously, the idea of "breaking news"—for which a television or radio network would interrupt a scheduled show—was limited to only the most extreme or impactful happenings, such as the Hindenburg airship disaster, the assassination of John F. Kennedy, or a declaration of war. With the advent of 24-hour news, however, the bar on what constituted a "need to know right now" story was set much, much lower.

At first, the constant news coverage was a novelty. We would tune in here and there. But soon we found ourselves tuning in more frequently, and sticking around for extended periods. It was no longer enough to hear the salient points of a particular story, we remained engaged long after knowing the basic facts— often out of fear that we would miss a new wrinkle to or layer of a story.

Out of fear.

Fast forward a few decades and the news (as I have stated before) is everywhere, available to us at any time. And while viewing it may give us a feeling that we are more connected with the world, it is decreasing genuine connection in our own lives.

The function of news, its intended purpose, is to supply us with necessary information that will help us make good decisions—about our country, our community, politics, our personal lives, etc. To keep us abreast of what is happening outside the sphere of our own purview. It is meant to be utilitarian, and while it does not have to be dry—it can be interesting or even enjoyable—the primary objective of news is not to keep us "informed," but to provide us with the information we need to make decisions.

Unfortunately, much of what is considered "news" by many Americans is actually "opinion"—and they are either unable to make the distinction or uninterested in bothering.

Here is one way to identify the difference: If you are receiving information about what has happened or is currently happening, it is news. If it has not happened and someone is speculating on what might happen, it is opinion. Media companies have hooked most Americans by creating a treadmill of future potential anxieties. Watch the next real news story about a weather event, shooting, or political event and you will witness the same cycle.

- This is what happened. *(News)*
- This is what it means. *(Opinion)*
- Because of that, this might happen, and you'd better stay tuned to find out more. *(Opinion + Baiting)*
- Oh my goodness! This is what we just *further learned* about what happened, and *that* could mean *this* might also happen! You'd better stay tuned! *(Opinion + Sensationalism + Baiting)*
- Heaven help us! This is what the next expert says might happen! You'd best tune in tomorrow or else. *(Opinion + Sensationalism + Baiting + Hyperbole)*

The vast majority of what you watch on the news is not about what *did* happen, but rather about what it means and what else could happen (and rarely does.)

* * *

What do you need to know?

There is an enormous difference between what we are staying informed about and what we truly *need* to be informed about. So, what is important for us to know? That varies based on who you ask, and there are no fixed rules. But according to PBS Newshour, there are five main "values" to consider in determining the newsworthiness of a given story:[9a]

- Timeliness
- Proximity
- Conflict and Controversy
- Human Interest
- Relevance

Even if a story is deemed "newsworthy," does that mean that *you* truly *need* to know it? Will it improve your life in some way, or help you make better decisions? Does it provide you with actionable information? The following topics and types of stories do:

- **Local (or relevant) Weather.** Depending on where you live, you might be able to accurately predict most weather based on previous experience, recalling the previous day, or looking out the window. For many of us, even if we cannot calculate or do not know the weather, it will have a negligible impact on our day. Some, though, live in extreme or highly unpredictable locations in terms of weather. In those cases, it may make more sense to utilize an app or alert service, rather than gather weather information from "the news."

- **Impending Disaster Warnings.** Avalanches, droughts, earthquakes, fires, flash floods, heat waves, ice storms, landslides, tornadoes, tropical cyclones, tsunamis, volcanic eruptions, etc. If one of these is headed your way, that is must-know information. However, in most areas, there are intricate alert systems designed to notify you in the event of disasters that could impact your location.

- **Proximate Attacks and Wars.** Information about conflicts that involve your country, or that are close to your vicinity, is important. This is rare. You can rest assured that critical elements of this type of information will find their way to you rather than you needing to seek them out.

- **Severe Government Abuse of Power or Corruption.** What is considered "severe" is subjective, but I would argue that 95%+ of political news does not fall into this category.

- **Local Crime** *(sort of)*. If there is a rash of robberies in your location, or a series of attacks, that would be helpful to know in terms of making decisions that impact the safety of you, your family, and your community. But it is important to remember that news is often driven by the edict "If it bleeds, it leads." A crime of passion between a husband and wife is considered a "hot" news item, and it may (sadly) boost ratings, but it has no significant impact on your life.

- **Traffic and Roads.** This is another category that, depending on where you live, you can predict to some degree. Those of us who live in busy metropolitan areas might need traffic info to determine the best route to work in the morning, but you can look up that information directly, or receive it via GPS, rather than tune in and wait for it on the news. However, in the case of a mudslide taking out a section of a back road or a wildfire shutting down a highway, yes—news about that would be helpful if it impacts your route(s).

- **Health Emergencies.** Another rare occurrence, but in the case of a pandemic (or potential pandemic), news outlets can provide some essential information.

Of the list above, what information could you get more accurately and quickly from the internet or an online app? Weather, disaster warnings, traffic, and health emergencies. The manipulation, sensationalism, and time involved in television news makes it, in my estimation, worth neither the risk nor the cost.

Even in the case of a pandemic, there is usually little need to stay glued to the television for hours on end. Think about the COVID-19 outbreak in early 2020. Most of us found ourselves attached to news coverage, at least at the beginning of the pandemic. Did that help us? Did continuous monitoring of that news give us a leg up in the pandemic (beyond what checking in for a few minutes daily would have)? Consider whatever news stories you currently have swirling about in your mind—do they provide you with actionable information? Perhaps. But probably not.

* * *

Infotainment and
Orchestrated Outrage

Think about the news you currently consume. If 5% of it is relevant and provides necessary, actionable information, what is the other 95% comprised of?

There is a word for it: *"Infotainment."*

Also known as "soft news," infotainment is a form of delivery that is meant to be as entertaining as informative (or, often, more so). "Time on-screen" is the key performance indicator (KPI) used by networks, cable, internet, streaming services, and social media, so the goal of infotainment is to keep you engaged and "plugged in" as long as possible. The more time you spend watching their programing, the more advertising they sell. The more advertising they sell, the more money they make.

So, what keeps people engaged? While few of us can resist a feel-good human interest story, it is not likely to hold our interest for very long.

But *fear* will.

As I said before, producers are very aware of the impulses of our ancient brain, and they know exactly how to influence it to their advantage. The purpose of news is to provide actionable information: If the content you are watching is not doing that, there is a good chance it is manipulating your emotions— influencing you, by design.

Many news outlets have become merchants of human misery. They know the best way to keep you on their screen is to make you believe they have information about a threat to you, your values, your loved ones, your community, your way of life . . . your "tribe."

"Is a common product in your home slowly killing you? Tune in at eleven."

Fear is lucrative. If these so-called news organizations cannot offer you a credible threat, they create one. **They know exactly how to orchestrate outrage to boost their bottom line.**

The fact is, bad news gets more attention, more clicks, and leads to more revenue for the publication.

KENT CAMPBELL

"Is the government trying to keep you from casting your ballot? Full story at six."

We cannot resist! We tune in because our protective instincts have kicked in. Then we notice the "crawl"—the scrolling headlines at the bottom of the screen—and additional impulses begin to fire. We stay tuned in because they've promised us more, and we feel a fundamental need to stay one step ahead of the perceived "threats."

The more we consume, the worse we feel—about ourselves, our future, our fellow citizens, our country, and the world. This only feeds our addiction to fear.

Some fears are universal, but others are split right down party lines. If you have ever wondered why we are seeing increased news organizations openly veering right or left politically, *that is why*. Because fear is profitable, and they are cashing in on a niche market.

If you genuinely want to be informed, it's important not only to consider what *kind* of news you are consuming but also *from where*. Media bias is alive and well in the United States. And while these outlets might not provide news that is *inaccurate*, much of it is very heavily one-sided—leaving out relevant bits of information that might not resonate with their chosen demographic.

Consider, too, that by narrowing their target market they can trigger fears more effectively. "They're coming to take your guns" is not as likely to stir outrage on a *left*-leaning network, but it works like a charm for those leaning *right*. On the flip-side, a *right*-leaning channel wouldn't use environmental threats to generate viewership, but for a *left*-leaning station, it could be a veritable gold mine.

Think about the sources you regularly consume news from, then open a web browser and search "Media Bias Ratings." Where do your sources fall on the left-to-right spectrum?

One of the best things you can do, after *limiting the amount* of news you consume, and *avoiding infotainment*, is to make a concerted effort to attain news *only* from sources shown to be unbiased.

* * *

You are the Product

Trust me when I tell you—you are a hot commodity. Whenever possible, troves of demographic and behavioral information are being gathered on you (on all of us) so that we can be "packaged" and sold to advertisers. And while you might think it's merely your attention that is for sale, they are buying much more of you than that.

Jaron Lanier, founder of VPL Research and author of *Ten Arguments for Deleting Your Social Media Accounts Right Now*, explains it well: "It's the gradual, slight, imperceptible change in your own behavior and perception that is the product.... That's the only thing there is for them to make money from. Changing what you do, how you think, who you are."[9b]

Sure, the end goal is for you to purchase their products or services. But what happens if you do not *want* or *need* a particular product or service? Simple. They *create* that need. This can be done by (for want of a better term) pulling on our emotional "levers." Some of these tools of manipulation include:

- **Fear.** *The old standby. This emotion, as you know, can be very compelling. One of the most common utilization methods is to simply create the fear of a missed opportunity (think "Limited Edition" or low inventory).*

- **Empathy.** *By presenting us with something we can relate to, brands make us feel heard and understood. They not only demonstrate the need for whatever product or service will solve the problem we are empathizing with, that sense of "they get me" may create brand loyalty in us as well.*

- **Guilt or Remorse.** *This is a trigger often used by charitable organizations, and I am sure I do not have to explain how it works in that regard. But these feelings can also push us to purchase products and services (think "sustainably sourced" or "environmentally friendly").*

- **Greed.** *We can pretend this will not work on us, but even the kindest and most charitable people I know are inspired by greed from time to time. It is not always an overt sense of "I want it all": more often we are triggered by the opportunity to get more than we are paying for (think "free gift with purchase" or "buy one, get one").*

- **Urgency.** *Creating a sense of time-sensitivity is an easy decision and goes hand-in-hand with fear. We are easily sucked in by statements such as "for a limited time only," "flash sale," "first come, first served," or "your cart will expire in 14 minutes."*

- **Belonging.** *We are lured into a sense of belonging by brands every day—and once we are committed, we can be fiercely loyal (think Pepsi vs. Coke, Ford vs. Chevy). Cola and cars have nothing to do with fashion, and yet we see people wearing these brand names on their clothing. They may feel more like community members than customers. Stirring our tribalistic instincts can be highly profitable.*

In the past, when we purchased newspaper and news magazine subscriptions (based on timeliness and quality), the *news* was the focus. Sure, there was advertising, but it was secondary to the articles and information. That is because we were their customers.

But as more news organizations took to the internet, things began to shift. I still remember the first time I realized I could access articles from one of my favorite news magazines online and free of charge. I was excited, but I could not help but wonder: Can they really afford to give this content away?

The answer is no. No, of course not. It is a business, and even newspapers and magazines that have phased out their print editions still have reporters, editors, executives, designers, marketers, photographers, administrators, and more to pay.

The question becomes *who will pay for the news?*

One by one, we've watched as outlets ranging from the *Wall Street Journal* to *Entertainment Weekly* wrestled with "paywall" strategies. We the people value quality reporting and accurate information, so we'll be willing to pay for online subscriptions, right? Maybe not.

As noted in *Fortune* magazine, "News consumers have become accustomed to free access to news content. Since we've been spoiled by news content that is available for free, we expect it to continue to be free."[9c]

> **"**
>
> *If you are not paying for it, you're not the customer; you're the product being sold.*
>
> ANDREW LEWIS

And so, the flip. For many news outlets, *advertisers* have become the customer, and readers are now—you guessed it—*the product.* In this model, the news itself is merely a means to an end. The bait if you will.

"That's fine," you might say. "I don't mind seeing ads when I read the news if it keeps the content free." But you might not be seeing the full picture. *When the news becomes bait, the question becomes "What bait is best?"*

At first it was just the headlines that changed, tweaked here and there to elicit a more emotional response. Whereas the function of a headline *used* to be summarizing the story below, it is now more a tool of enticement. Therefore, we often hear cries of *"Did you even read the article?"* What the headline implies and what the story explains may be quite different.

The adjustments didn't stop with titles, however. Soon something else became clear—that it was not just about luring you to a story, it was about *keeping you on the page.* The longer you stay, the more they get paid. So many news outlets began to sensationalize the stories themselves, in addition to the headlines, and give preference to stories of a negative nature. Some became masters at *appearing* to say something false without saying it. Others just blatantly began to misrepresent the facts—embellishing, dramatizing, or overstating along the way. The more negative, the better.

We pay more attention to bad news than good. This is because humans have a *negativity bias*, and unpleasant stimuli tend to have a stronger impact on our minds. (This is why, at the end of the day; we often forget the twenty-seven *good* things that happened to us and focus on the one *bad* thing that happened.)

This isn't learned behavior, either. Studies have shown that even infants display negative bias.[9d] It's encoded in our ancient brains. And like so many other instincts, it's mostly about survival.

Imagine one of your ancestors walking through a forest. If they come across a snake and a butterfly, obviously the snake is going to get more of their attention. It activates their stress response. Their brain tells them to pay heed so they can take appropriate steps to ensure their safety. Those with this instinct were more likely to survive, and those who survived passed along their instincts genetically. So, humans are constantly on guard for threats—relentlessly focusing on the negative. *And newsmakers know it.*

"Negative news catches our attention, captures our imagination, and scares us into reading more, because negativity looms larger in the human brain than positive events," said *USA Today* columnist Jeff Stibel. "We are controlled by our emotions, and our emotions are controlled by fear. A tiny almond-shaped part of our brain called the amygdala drives all of this. Even though it's small, the amygdala can override our decision-making, and is hyper-tuned to negativity. Inside the amygdala, a single negative event makes roughly the same impression as five positive events."[9e]

Bad news sells because the amygdala is always looking for something to fear.

PETER DIAMANDIS

Journalistically speaking, *when news is bad, business is good.*

Those who would profit from our penchant for negativity take what they know about our cognitive biases and tribalistic instincts, combine that with the hot button issue *du jour*, toss in a bit of dramatization, and top it off with a particularly sensational headline. The result? We're made to believe that even benign topics are a matter of life and death, and we can't get enough of it. They're hijacking our survival mechanisms for their own gain.

Our increased anger about political issues makes for an easy target. If you are regularly scared of, outraged by, and hateful towards half of America, *you're being manipulated.* Period. The "other side" is not your enemy—but your news source very well might be.

One of the best ways to identify a credible news source is to look for relatively dull reporting. (Seriously.) Real, truthful, accurate news is generally quite dry. *That's as it should be.* If you want entertainment, read a novel. If you want information, look for the flavorless purity of journalistic integrity.

Considering how vastly different the resulting articles can be, it often surprises people to learn that there are two major news "wholesalers" in the United States supplying core content to all of the major outlets. (This includes, but is not limited to: CNN, MSNBC, CNBC, Fox News, ABC, NBC, CBS, and just about every news radio show in America.) They are:

- The Associated Press (www.apnews.com)
- Reuters News (www.reuters.com)

They provide the facts, the outlets provide the spin (if any), and I'm constantly amazed at how the same story can be portrayed so differently depending on where I'm reading it. For that reason, and because I want to be informed--not influenced—I often go straight to AP or Reuters.

If you're not used to getting your news from one of these sources, do me a favor and go visit one of them now. Open the site and spend a few minutes there.

If you have become accustomed to over-sensationalized news, you're going to find AP and Reuters to be *incredibly boring.* First, you will scan the headlines—and notice that you've had a chance to scan several because nothing grabbed your attention in a way that made you feel an urgent need to click through. Then you will select a story and begin reading . . . and within a few moments, your mind might begin to wander. Without dramatization and a tribal political slant—in the absence of propagandizing—you have little emotional interest in the story.

This remarkable difference should reveal just how manipulative the media you've been consuming can be. News outlets are inventing and increasing discord by creating exaggerated, misleading, and sometimes slanderously false stories to keep you engaged and keep themselves in business. The net effect is that the average American is anxious, scared, outraged, and might believe that our country's survival is dependent upon eliminating the "other side."

Media companies have become merchants of division.

If a news outlet is constantly telling you what you want to hear, you're being manipulated. It's time to *stop being their product* and find another source. It isn't the job of the news to ease your mind or stoke your emotions with headlines, editorial choices, or source curation. News should simply inform us of what is happening—based on verifiable facts, and with proper context—reporting information fully and fairly. Whether that comforts you, scares you, delights you, or enrages you should be up to you, *and it should not be for sale.*

* * *

Addicted to "Outrage Porn"

Our consumption of news has gotten out of hand. No one, and I mean *no one*, needs to remain glued to a 24/7 news network, 24/7. It isn't healthy, and it isn't helpful. Yet, that's just what many Americans are doing.

A dear friend of mine (we'll call her "Mary") recently returned from visiting her parents' home. She knew I was drafting this book and wanted to share her story—in hopes that it might help to illustrate just how dreadful things have gotten for some.

The entire time Mary was visiting, if her father was not at work, he was seated in an armchair directly in front of the television. He rose hours before dawn to watch, immediately returned to his chair after work, and remained there long past midnight. Mary began to wonder if her father ever really *did* go to bed, because when she rose in the middle of the night, there he was—still perched in front of the glowing blue screen, leaned in, eyes wide, staring intently, a blanket gripped tightly beneath his chin with both fists.

He wasn't just casually watching, and that's what struck Mary the most. She told me "he looked as though he had seen a ghost." His face was pale, he was tense, stiff, and his knuckles were white from the sheer force of his grip on that blanket.

All this behavior would be alarming on its own, but Mary soon discovered that the problems didn't end when her father left his easy chair. He was listening to radio news on his commute as well, and multiple times each day he would call home to complain about a newspaper article, video, or online commentary.

According to Mary's mother, this was nothing new. This was normal. The news had consumed him, and it was taking over their lives. It had gotten so out of hand, in fact, that Mary's mother was talking about leaving. Mary wondered, too, how long his employer would be able to put up with his addiction.

I'd love to be able to tell you that Mary's story isn't true—that it's just a work of fiction to augment my book—but, sadly, it is neither fabricated nor exaggerated. Sadder still, Mary's father is not alone. Countless Americans live a similar existence, suffering from *fear-driven information addiction.* Although it sounds counter-intuitive, fear releases dopamine—and whenever there is a cheap, abundant source of dopamine you'll find addiction. People are addicted to feeling fear, turning social media, cable, and internet television into "outrage porn" delivery machines.

Move over baseball, news is the new national pastime.

When you saw the title of this chapter, you might have confidently thought to yourself, "No, that's not me. I'm not addicted to fear and hate." Maybe you prefer to avoid anything that creates an adrenaline rush, like thrill rides, heights, or horror movies. But those are *selective* fears: situations you chose (or not) to involve yourself in that induce a mild fear response.

Feeling involuntarily fearful, enraged, or defensive due to our primitive behavioral instincts is a bit different. We are investigative gratification seekers. When we recognize a potential catastrophe, we can't help but dig deeper. We feel the need to wrap our heads around it to maintain control and to survive.

But giving in to these impulses means we're continuously exposed to negative information, which can have a severe physical and psychological impact on us.

* * *

Your Cheater Detection Mechanism

The human brain can be thought of as a computer—an organic one, designed to process information in adaptive ways. It is comprised of many programs, each of which was good at solving either a survival or reproduction problem faced by our ancient ancestors. The *cheater detection mechanism* is one of these programs in our internal operating system, and its objective is to discover fraud in situations involving social exchange.

Whenever you trade favors, purchase goods, or help someone who has helped you, you engage in social exchange—cooperation for mutual benefit. The idea is simple enough: I provide you with something of value, you reciprocate, and we are both better off. Evolutionary biologists demonstrated that social exchange cannot evolve in a species unless those who engage in it can identify cheaters—that is, individuals who take benefits from others without providing them in return. Psychologists discovered that humans have a built-in detection "mechanism" (or brain function) for this. We are constantly on the lookout for companies, organizations, movements, or people who may be "cheating" us or, by extension, society. When these charlatans are identified, the injustice makes our proverbial blood boil. Depending on our tribal affiliation, our perception of what constitutes an "injustice" can be vastly different.

The detection mechanism for those on one end of the political spectrum might have been triggered in recent years by:

- *Children separated from their parents at the border*

- *The Muslim ban*

- *President Trump*

Those on the opposite end might have been triggered by:

- *Providing healthcare to illegal immigrants*

- *Tax increases*

- *President Obama*

And both sides were outraged, for different reasons, by:

- *Tom Brady*

News outlets and media personalities not only look for issues that will trip our cheater detection mechanisms but, once found, they will amplify, exaggerate, and provide unending coverage. Why? Because it helps them improve their most important metric—"time on screen." Keep in mind that the more time you spend angrily watching, the more advertising they sell, and the more profitable their business becomes.

What happens when there's not enough blood-boiling domestic news? Networks may turn to local or isolated stories that they can magnify and "nationalize." Small local issues can be highlighted and positioned in a way that makes them appear relevant to a wider audience, and producers know it. Remember, also, that informing you isn't what's profitable—the profit is in the advertising, and the payout depends on your addiction to their "screen."

If your news channel of choice or favorite media personality always seems to be jumping from one outrage to the next, keeping you constantly in a state of anxiety or agitation, *you're a pawn in their game.*

* * *

It's not funny.

So, what about relatively light-hearted news programs, late-night comedy, or satirical news sources? Surely these are exempt from concern. Surely this isn't "negative" information?

Think again.

Americans enjoy turning to programs like these to wind down in the evening, or even as a form of catharsis—laughing at the very events that have weighed heavily on them throughout the day. But while the hosts often discuss lighter topics, entertainment, or snappier news stories, they also spend a great deal of time and energy focusing on politics and current events. And while these subjects might be broached in a lighthearted, comedic fashion, our brains are deciphering. **We're subconsciously seeking out and absorbing the negativity.**

Even in the case of well-intentioned humor regarding a political leader, the "jokes" are altering our opinions and transforming our relationship with that leader. We may slowly come to view them as someone to laugh at and ridicule, rather than to respect and cooperate with.

No matter how soaked in humor, satire, and good intentions a program might be, the effect is the same—increased anxiety, arrogance, and divisiveness.

* * *

How bad is your addiction?

Short quiz....

- How much news do you consume, on average, per day?

  _____

- How do you consume it? (*Cable, radio, articles, etc.*)

  _____

- What subjects do you focus on?

  _____

- Do these topics upset you? (*Anxiety, anger, fear, etc.*)

  _____

- Do you share the information with others?
  (*If so, how and how often?*)

  _____

- What do you do if someone questions what you've shared or doesn't take it as seriously as you do?

  _____

When most of us hear the word "news," we think of current events or political updates. Many of us would argue against our addiction to these subjects, but we're failing to consider the other news topics we're more likely to consume daily. As a species, we have a primal desire to stay informed about what's going on around us—and a fear of missing out (FOMO). From checking in on community happenings to keeping up with the Kardashians, we're willing to exchange copious amounts of our time for the latest information on whatever subject(s) we happen to be tracking. The impact of this can be both physiological (sore neck, worsened eyesight) and psychological (decreased empathy, shorter attention spans). But when we become addicted to *political* news, other (often bigger) concerns come into play.

Most of us begin tracking political news when we feel something is at stake, such as needing better healthcare after receiving an impossible diagnosis, dealing with the impact of mounting student loan debt, or having any hot button issue suddenly hit close to home. Once we are emotionally invested, it becomes difficult (if not impossible) to look away.

National crises often spark information addiction, too. According to Scott L. Althaus, increasing our news consumption during a time of national crisis or personal conflict is a common phenomenon. Sometimes the shift is due to an individual's desire to be involved and to help fellow citizens, but because watching the news can provide us with the *illusion* of making a difference, we might not take any real action. Althaus explains, "Changing levels of civic-mindedness are likely to be seen first in lower-cost behaviors, like paying attention to the news, before they are seen in higher-cost activities, like by volunteering or joining a group."[9f]

When we begin to actively consume political news out of what feels like necessity, we embrace the routine because it produces a false sense of control. In our democracy, we can vote on elected officials, but we have little involvement in how those who have been elected will handle issues at hand. It's really nothing more than a spectator sport, but tracking the news daily, or multiple times per day, or through multiple sources, creates for us the feeling of influence and involvement that we desperately crave.

Once a behavior like this feels obligatory—as if it were our patriotic duty to stay "well-informed"— it is much more difficult to reason or converse with

While television is a good servant, it's a bad master. It can swallow up huge quantities of our lives without much happiness bang for the buck.

GRETCHEN RUBIN

us. Those who focus on political news, major political figures, and others' political affiliations are often struggling with highly addictive, psychological fixations which can be damaging to themselves, their relationships, our nation, and the world. Not only are many losing relationships over political differences, but we're also harming our health along the way—developing or increasing anxiety, depression, anger, and apathy.

CHAPTER TEN

DECONSTRUCTION

OF A

FEARMONGER

"A culture cannot lie down with dogs
and not become utterly infested with fleas.
The dogs, in this case, are the mongrel media
and the corporate overlords who have
grown fat on manufactured controversy
and fear-mongering."

STEVEN WEBER
American Actor

T here are many reasons why someone might derive a sense of gratification from fear, but most of it boils down to *vigilance*. Our focus on the negative stems from a deeply encoded instinct to remain vigilant as a means of avoiding harm, and our neurochemical processes reinforce this. It is an ancient process that has served us well in terms of evolution and survival, but one that is highly susceptible to manipulation. Those who would harness these instincts to influence our thoughts and behaviors are *fearmongers*.

Fearmongering involves hijacking our brain's most primal impulses as a means of control, and it is incredibly dangerous—both individually and collectively. Not only can it cause us to grossly miscalculate risk, but it can also misdirect our attention in a way that leaves us quite vulnerable. (If our attention is focused on a manufactured fear, we may be missing actual threats to our safety.)

This effect is not lost on politicians and political parties. You've heard the term "smoke and mirrors" bandied about in recent years—the idea that a politician has brought one problem to the forefront to direct our attention away from another. This tactic is real, and (unfortunately) can be remarkably effective.

Our fear can also be used to rally support. When we perceive an external fear, we may be more likely to support a leader or their policies. The Nazi Party, for example, sought to convince German citizens that war was the only way to save the country from its external enemies. The result was one of the darkest and most deadly chapters in world history.

Someone experiencing fear might not be able to think clearly or critically, and their decision-making skills can suffer. In this state, we might be more willing to allow someone to do our thinking for us—to rely more heavily on the advice of a leader. (If you're thinking, "Surely I wouldn't fall victim to this," just picture yourself trapped in a dark alley, surrounded by gunmen. Suddenly you hear a voice whisper, "Follow me! I know a way out!" What would you do?)

Our fear can lead us to follow blindly and give up control. This is bad enough on an individual level, but collective fear is especially dangerous. *If you've ever read a history book and wondered why so many people were willing to go along with some horrible act, collective fear is likely the reason.*

* * *

Five trademarks of a fearmonger

Fearmongers come in all shapes and sizes, and their motives are extremely varied, but today most of them just want fame and fortune. They are profiting on your fear, outrage, and the division of the nation. Here are some tell-tale "trademarks" which will help you identify a fearmonger. (In the descriptions below, "party" refers to whomever/whatever might be fearmongering—be that a person, organization, political party, news outlet, etc.)

1: PURVEYOR AND PROTECTOR

If the party *telling* you about the fear is also claiming they're best suited to *protect* you from it, *they might be fearmongering.*

In this scenario, the fearmonger will induce fears and phobias, and in the same breath suggest that the only way to avoid the dire consequences of these is through the fearmonger or by heeding their advice. They offer both hazard and help, first inventing (or at least exaggerating) a problem or villain, then portraying themselves as the superhero best suited to save you.

The manufactured fear is merely a means to an end. Getting you to buy this idea of them as a "savior" is the goal. They need you to believe, seek comfort, and put your trust in them, and they'll push the idea that their only concern is for your best interests.

Watch out for phrases such as:

- *"I want you to know the truth."*
- *"I've got your back."*
- *"You know who is looking out for you."*

This type of fearmongering can feel like an emotional rollercoaster. First, we are presented with a fear, then we are made to feel protected from it, then the cycle begins again.

2: THE THREAT OF "THEY"

If a party is constantly focused on vilifying a competitor or opponent, or dividing you from them and their supporters, *they are fearmongering.*

While there is certainly no shortage of threats out there, and plenty of well-intentioned people who might warn us about them, I question the motives of anyone who continuously attempts to paint their direct competition or opposition as the sole or primary threat.

Watch out for phrases such as:

- *"They want you to think...."*
- *"They don't care about you."*
- *"They're scared of us."*
- *"They want to destroy the country that we love so much."*
- *"They're the enemy of the people."*

This trademark tactic is used by politicians and media personalities alike.

3: OVERSIMPLIFICATION AND JARGON

If a party is dramatically oversimplifying complex problems, boiling them down into easy, bite-sized, "common sense" solutions, *they might be fearmongering.*

When this tactic is employed, all nuance, empathy, or complete understanding of the situation is lost. Complicated situations and scenarios might be reduced to only a few words, shutting down our critical thinking and causing *intellectual laziness.*

The fearmonger might also create their own jargon or catchphrases. Utilizing these expressions can be a powerful symbol of tribal allegiance and create a sense of camaraderie (and exclusivity). Talking to outsiders who don't understand this terminology can become tedious and awkward. Some, feeling left out, might want to learn what these words and mottos mean, drawing them in and making them "one of us." If not, they become outsiders, and we might separate ourselves from them because they "just don't understand." This only serves the fearmonger, as it distances us from those who could offer an unfamiliar perspective.

4: ELITISM AND SUPERIORITY

If a party continually portrays themselves as special—as uniquely and exclusively virtuous—and implies that through following them you, by extension, will also be special, *they might be fearmongering.*

The overwhelming majority of humans are not malevolent. Those who hold different beliefs and opinions do so out of a genuine feeling that those values are "right" or in the best interest of society. So when it is suggested that one group holds the patent on morality, righteousness, or intelligence—we should be suspicious.

The fearmonger *wants* us to feel special and included—a valued member of an elite group that is going to, for example, change history, save the world, or improve humankind in some way. They want you to feel collectively powerful, and there is a powerful sense of mission and purpose that binds the group together and keeps them working diligently to achieve their goals. This sense of elitism often causes participants to feel superior to those outside of the group. This gives rise to an interesting contradiction: while followers are reliable and humble before the fearmonger, they can be disobedient and arrogant to outsiders.

Fearmongering works because we allow it to: we play our part in the cycle of fear, blame, and hatred.

ABDUL EL-SAYED

This loyalty serves the fearmonger well. The sense of entrusted power and responsibility (to save the country, for example), can lead us to feelings of guilt if we're not participating, watching, voting, protesting, or fighting when the fearmonger wants us to be.

5: JUSTIFIED VIOLENCE

If a party is encouraging you to excuse or support violence, based on the (self-proclaimed) significance of their objective, *they might be fearmongering.*

The fearmonger will encourage followers to dismiss lying, cheating, aggression, and brutality as justifiable means to an end because they are (or want you to believe they are) doing especially important things (e.g. protecting the "soul" of the nation, exposing corruption in others).

In fact, to manipulate us into tolerating (or participating in) their corruption and scheming, they might portray their competitor(s) or opponent(s) as the corrupt or scheming party. If they can sell you that story, then any protest, riot, or violence perpetrated by them or their followers is justifiable and patriotic, while the same acts committed by "the other side" become proof of their craven, ruthless, lawless, and unpatriotic ways.

CHAPTER ELEVEN

FIGHT THE FEARMONGER

"Ignorance leads to fear,
fear leads to hatred,
and hatred leads to violence.
This is the equation."

IBN RUSHD
Philosopher and Theologian

T he fearmonger is here to stay. Its weapons will continue to aim in our direction whether we like it or not, and a counterattack would be ineffective, at least on the individual level. *So, what can we do to fight back?*

Think of the fearmonger's ammunition like a poison dart. What's the best way to protect yourself from injury? I suggest a two-pronged approach: try to avoid getting hit, and build up an immunity for when it's unavoidable.

Be your own curator. Take control, whenever possible, of your information consumption. *Go to it,* on your terms, rather than constantly leaving yourself open for *it* to find *you.* Be cautious and deliberate about which source(s) you will accept information from and which you won't. Be purposeful, too, about what sort of knowledge you will seek out, how, and how often. When faced with news or information, especially if it elevates your heart rate, ask yourself, *Did I invite this or is it invading?*

Check for impact and usefulness. Try to be mindful of what information is important and purposeful versus that which is useless (or even harmful). Ask yourself, *Does this impact me? Is it useful? Is there anything I can do about it? Is there anything actionable here?*

Gauge your reaction. There are high integrity, truthful news items and bits of information that will raise our blood pressure, but pay attention to whether your concern comes from a genuine place or if it might be *intentionally sparked fear.* Ask yourself, *Is this something I was (or would have been) concerned about before reading/hearing this information?*

The last two paragraphs and bits of advice go together, and they're important to consider any time you consume news or information. I use the acronym "AIR" as a reminder to stop, breathe, and....

<u>A</u>ssess <u>I</u>mpact, <u>R</u>eaction. (A.I.R.)

A tsunami warning in your area, for example, could spark fear in you, but rightly so. That news impacts you, contains useful information, and yes—there are things you can (and should) do about it. But a "news" story about how the politician you already don't like made a comment you find distasteful—is that worth your time? Is it helpful? Is it worth getting physically worked up over?

Avoid the steaming headline. As I mentioned before, genuine (non-sensationalized) news is often boring, and headlines should quickly and briefly summarize the story below (not have an opinion or get your blood boiling). When the headline alone immediately sparks fear or gets your heart beating faster, there's a good chance it is baiting you. First thing's first, *stop* and try to control any knee-jerk reactions. Ask yourself, *Is this dramatized, leading, or exaggerated? Did this spark anger and fear, or genuine interest? If I'm concerned about this topic, what's the best source for me to learn more about it?*

That last bit of advice is golden, at least for me. Often, despite our best efforts to avoid them, we come across particularly sensationalized headlines meant to lure us in. I will feel my heart rate quicken, begin to get angry, but I try to stop myself, breathe, and "A.I.R." it out. If I'm still interested in learning more about the topic, I *do not click through.* Instead, I try to determine where I can find the best, *most accurate* information on the subject.

Fact. Check. Everything.

We must always be mindful that what we are hearing might be misleading, incomplete, out of context, inaccurate, or flat-out lies.

The term "fake news" has become quite common in the last few years, however the definition changes drastically depending on who you ask. In general, it is false or misleading information that is passed off as being factual. Sensationalism, negativism, and fearmongering are the "Holy Trinity" of fake news.

Consumption of "fake news" is more serious than simply being ill-informed (though that is bad enough). Depending on the content, our relationships with others could be damaged, and important decisions (such as who we'll vote for) might be in jeopardy. We can also experience heightened levels of anxiety, anger, fear, hatred, resentment, and depression. While over-exposure to factual news can cause some of the same effects, the impacts are much more immediate, drastic, and difficult to reverse when we're subjected to a steady stream of lies, half-truths, and clickbait.

All information is guilty until proven innocent.

A. D. ALIWAT

Before you accept new information, ask yourself:

- *Is this true?*
- *Is this biased?*
- *Is this complete?*
- *Is this logical?*

If you have *any* doubts—if you see a single red flag—please *fact-check* that information. Trust me when I tell you that even sources considered to be accurate, fair, balanced, and objective can mislead (or just get it wrong) sometimes. *The best tool in our arsenal is our own due diligence.*

* * *

Homework: Track your consumption

The advice above is important, and I hope you will take it to heart and use it regularly. What follows below are steps you can take right now. Your "assignment" for the week if you will:

LIMIT YOUR TIME

Throughout the next week, maintain a record of your exposure to the news. This includes televised news, late-night comedy shows, articles and videos on social media, newspapers, magazines, and word of mouth. Write down the approximate number of minutes you engaged with the news and the venue through which you accessed it.

DATE	SOURCE	TIME SPENT

You might be surprised to see how much time you spend interacting with the news, and what sources your information is coming from. A friend told me she normally got her news from the *Economist* and *NPR* and spent about 1-2 hours per week consuming news. After doing this exercise, she discovered that most of her weekly information intake was from scrolling social media—where she had little control over the sources. She was also shocked to see just how much idle time she spent browsing headlines or getting sucked into time-wasting, inconsequential stories. That 1-2 hours she estimated ended up being closer to 10-15. She resolved to limit her access, set time limits, and even delete a couple of apps from her phone.

Once your week is up, and you have carefully documented your intake, consider the following:

- How much time did you spend consuming news?
- How did you access it?
- How do you feel about that?
- What changes do you want to make, in terms of:
  - *The ways you access news?*
  - *The frequency?*
  - *The time you spend consuming it?*

EVALUATE YOUR SOURCES

While you were recording your news consumption, you might have noticed also that you were more drawn to some news sources than others. Consider why this is: do they write more news stories that interest you, do you like their writing style, do you trust them, or are they representing your political party?

Revisit your news consumption tracker, and consider the following questions:

- What news sources did you access this week?
- Did you choose these sources, or did some choose you?
- What types of content do they post? (Are they a news channel, or do they cover entertainment, etc.?)
- Do you feel all the sources were legitimate?
- Look at their "About" pages. How does each appear to be affiliated?
- Look at an up-to-date media bias chart. Where do they each fall on the left-right spectrum?

If your news source appears to be affiliated with a particular political party (e.g., Democrats), visit a website of another party (e.g., Republicans) that has covered that same news story. Does the story look or feel different to you depending on the party affiliation?

Note: if you are struggling to tell the difference between legitimate and fake sources, do your research. Perform a quick search online, asking if a website is legit. You will find ample reviews if it is a source to be aware of. As for troll accounts, consider "Spot the Bot" and similar straight-forward training that will teach you in under five minutes how to tell the difference.

CHECK THE FACTS

Look back on your tracker answers and consider the following questions:

- How did they do on headlines? Were you baited?
- Did you feel the news you consumed was all reasonably well reported, fair, balanced, and accurate?
- Did the information presented have sources cited?

- Did you fact-check anything? If so, how did they do in terms of representing the facts?

For anything you didn't fact check, check it now, just for your own edification. Consider also comparing news stories you read to those on the same topic presented by a different source. Is anything contradictory, or does the information appear to be consistent?

* * *

Consider Cutting Back (or Eliminating)

It's a promising idea to carefully curate your news sources, and it might also be a promising idea to consider cutting back on your news intake in general. There are ample benefits to this, including:

- **More time**
  I've dropped my average screen time from 4 hours per day to just 2. If I keep it up, I'm saving over 700 hours (about 4 weeks) per year!

- **Improved mood**
  I am far happier now that I have reduced my news consumption, and when I do access the news, I no longer suffer from a hair-trigger temper.

- **Increased compassion, understanding**
  I'm discovering a new comprehension on many issues, and I find that these days it is much easier for me to project myself

into the shoes of others, to consider the other "side" of an issue.

- **Decreased fear and anger**
  Through this work—and by remembering to stop, breathe, and "AIR" things out—I've managed to eliminate the "blood boiling" frustration I used to experience. This is key because it was that rage and resentment that made me erroneously believe that we (Americans) would never be able to "get along."

- **Greater hope**
  Once I realized I was being manipulated, and took steps to correct that, the world began to look a little more hopeful. I came to see that our differences were not as vast as I had once thought.

- **More mindfulness**
  Between the reduction in time spent and the shift in what I was consuming (and how), I am now far more "present"—at the dinner table, social outings, dates, parties, and family gatherings. I show up completely, and I am fully in the moment.

- **Better connections**
  It might not be this way with you, but for me, conversations often began with "Did you hear about...." or "Can you believe...," followed by whatever news item had outraged me on that day. I now make a point to make my news consumption not only limited but personal. It is for me, and I leave others to determine where and how they consume news (I've removed myself as a source). This has led to far

better connections and far more meaningful and enjoyable
conversations. Instead of news or politics, I talk about:

- o *Entertainment*
- o *Children, grandchildren*
- o *Sports*
- o *Travel*
- o *Personal histories, stories*
- o *Humor, jokes*
- o *Amusing anecdotes*

This advice is not one-size-fits-all. You might already have your news consumption in check, and, if so, I applaud you. But if not, I hope you were able to learn some useful information by participating. I believe almost everyone (who hasn't already consciously and purposefully altered their news habits) has something to gain from this exercise.

Social Media:
Rage Against
the Outrage Machine

"I favor humans over ideology,
but right now the ideologues are winning,
and they're creating a stage for constant
artificial high dramas, where everyone is either
a magnificent hero or a sickening villain."

JON RONSON
American Journalist, Author, and Filmmaker

CHAPTER TWELVE

THE
ALGORITHM

*"Silo builds the wall in people's
minds and creates the barrier in
organizations' hearts."*

PEARL ZHU

Author, Digital Visionary

N o doubt you are aware of the crisis that began in
Myanmar (formerly known as Burma) in 2016, when the
government, aided by extremist monks, began
perpetrating acts of "ethnic cleansing" and genocide against the
Rohingya people. That's frightening enough, but what is more
terrifying is—*they did it with the help of social media.*

Many will tell you that, in Myanmar, Facebook "is" the
internet. While the web had technically been available since
2000, it was heavily censored. That censorship was partially
reduced beginning in 2011, but restrictions persisted. "During
the years of censorship, if you wanted to know what was going
on you had to go down to the tea shop and chat with people,"

explained independent political analyst Richard Horsey. "When Facebook came along, it gelled with that way of doing things—a digital tea shop."[12a]

Entering the country in 2010, the Facebook app became extremely popular because it could be used without incurring data charges. In fact, it came pre-loaded on mobile phones. Its reach in Myanmar was vast, and military operatives took advantage, exploiting the app's popularity to launch a deliberate and systemic campaign that would incite violence and sow division.

Military personnel trolled Facebook, creating phony pages and fake profiles, and used them to disseminate false narratives and propaganda. They created "news" pages and posed as models and pop stars to gain large followings. They studied metrics and shared fabricated stories, such as the rape of a Buddhist woman by a Muslim man. They spread rumors of violent acts or planned attacks—carefully timing posts to target key demographics. They deliberately planted, propagated, and escalated division and hatred, and, sadly, it worked. The details are horrific, and I won't share them here. Suffice it to say—the extreme power of social media had been

As information and voice amplification become the new symbols of power, those who would assume control of society have moved to hoard voice amplification and control the message received by the public in new ways.

HEATHER MARSH

proven. In the wrong hands, it was deadly. As Rin Fujimatsu, Advocacy Director of Progressive Voice, put it, "Facebook was complicit in a genocide."[12b]

It would be easy, or at least comfortable, to think that *we* could not so easily be manipulated—but it would also be naïve. We've already seen evidence of Russian tampering in our elections, and these sorts of misinformation campaigns are taking place in other countries, too. As *New York Times* reporter Alexandra Stevenson points out, "In some countries, Facebook's experiments have helped to amplify fake stories, while its slower response in other developing countries, including Sri Lanka, has allowed rumors to spark violence."[12c]

The grim reality is this: on social media we are marionettes, and our strings are already being pulled. The question is by whom, and to what end?

* * *

The internet—and, more specifically, social media—is our most connective modern tissue. But for a technology conceived as a means of connecting us, it has become surprisingly (and dangerously) divisive. We erroneously believed, early on, that it would have the opposite effect—bringing us closer together by expanding our understanding of and empathy for one another. And while that may have been true, for a time, it has since transformed into the world's largest stage for grandstanding, soapboxing, misleading, mocking, ridicule, harassment, propaganda, and public performance. *And anyone can audition for a leading role.*

When the Founding Fathers designed our country, division was a concern. But they (and James Madison) believed that the sheer size of the United States might be the antidote. The man who would be our fourth President was quoted as saying, "The influence of factious leaders may kindle a flame within their particular States but will be unable to spread a general conflagration through the other States."

Fast-forward a couple of centuries, and while the United States is even larger than our Founding Fathers imagined, it has been made quite small in terms of the potential reach of one person's power. In fact, we now have a name for it—"influencer." And while many self-described influencers are busy selling makeup, branded merchandise, fitness plans, and at-home meal prep kits, others have a much

> ## "
> *There are many things of which a wise man might wish to be ignorant.*
>
> RALPH WALDO EMERSON

darker agenda. Literally anyone with an internet connection could launch a movement, spread a conspiracy theory, or generate a disinformation campaign from the comfort of their home—creating extreme division and gaining hundreds of thousands of followers in the process.

* * *

The Programming Problem

There are two important lines of code that contribute very heavily to our growing problem of disunity. The first is the ancient tribalistic instinct encoded in our human brains. The second is *the algorithm*—one of the most impactful digital codes ever written. You see, while we are at the mercy of our ancient impulses, they have remained unchanged throughout human history. This allows us to understand them, and we can learn to exert a certain amount of control over them (with work, patience, and practice). The same cannot be said for the mysterious *algorithm*. Not only is it not publicly accessible, but most of us would have no earthly hope of comprehending it if it were. And even if we *were* all able to read and understand intricate lines of digital code, and even if that code *were* made public, we could never hope to fully understand the algorithm, because *it is constantly changing*.

The algorithm is a detailed formula that impacts everything we do and see on social media. It uses what it knows about us (our habits, behaviors, interests) to determine what types of content we are most likely to interact with, then uses that information to determine what we will see, where, when, and how often. You will notice I said that it delivers what we are "most likely to *interact* with," not what we "*most like*." That's a significant distinction.

What captures our attention is often driven by that other code—the one in our brains that I've covered (ad nauseam?) throughout the pages of this book. While the average American may like kittens and Muppet memes, nothing grabs and holds our attention like perceived threats and negativity.

The algorithm's purpose is to drive engagement. Whether that is to benefit the end-user or the advertiser, and to what degree, is not entirely certain. But we know that the algorithm is set up to benefit the social media platform itself, and we know that these platforms are businesses. As Peter Cashmore noted, *attention is the new currency*, and whether that attention is good, bad, healthy, or harmful doesn't much matter.

> **"**
>
> *Until you realize how easy it is for your mind to be manipulated, you remain the puppet of someone else's game.*
>
> EVITA OCHEL

The war for your attention is driving the brewing civil war, and social media is one of the major culprits.

* * *

The Persona Problem

It's not just what we interact with on social media, but *how* we interact that is a problem. It used to be that we would read a story in a newspaper, think about it, form an opinion, and either keep that opinion to ourselves or share it with a few people—a spouse, a friend, a coworker—by word of mouth. But in the world of social media, where opinions are quickly formed and published online, the opinion may not have had a reasonable amount of gestation time, and the audience isn't necessarily just a few trusted folks. Not only is that opinion etched in stone (if you don't already realize that something on the internet lives forever, you need to wrap your brain around that), but it's also subject to viewing and analysis by a much larger swath of people.

And so, what we post isn't necessarily genuine or authentic. Often it is influenced by thoughts such as:

- *How will this be taken by those who agree with me?*
- *How will this be taken by those who don't?*
- *How will this make me look to each of them?*
- *Will I be praised?*
- *Will I be criticized?*
- *Will I sound smart?*
- *Will I sound stupid?*

We know others will scrutinize, so we might first scrutinize ourselves. And all those questions are influenced by what result the poster wants. Perhaps they would like to appear bold and strong. Perhaps they prefer to come across as being sweet and thoughtful. Whatever persona they want to portray to the world must be considered, and it could be a significant departure from one's "real" personality.

When we interact face to face with those who know us personally to some degree, we are typically more humble, truthful, and respectful. There are many reasons for this, not the least of which being that we know they already *know* us, and we know we will have to interact with them again.

The same cannot be said for social media, where not only is there a false sense of anonymity (depending on where and how we're networking), but our inhibitions may be reduced due to the absence of physical interaction. There is a sense of "safety" when we type out a statement on a keyboard in a quiet bedroom, versus saying the same thing aloud to a group of people in the same room. This is largely because, when we're posting online, we don't have to look anyone in the eye or fully realize and acknowledge that there are real humans on the other "end" of things. But there's also a survival instinct involved. If we're

> *There are only two industries that refer to their customers as 'users', one is of course IT, the other is the illegal drugs trade.*
>
> EDWARD TUFTE

standing right in front of someone when we say something particularly hateful, there's a real possibility they'll react by socking us directly in the jaw.

When you think about those who frequently post their unrelenting support for that which you would spend your life opposing, you wonder how they could do such a thing. We've already covered tribalism and how our ancient instincts factor in, but the desire to mold and maintain a public persona could also be part of the equation. More specifically—pride could be part of the equation.

We all know someone who is so painfully prideful that they will not—cannot—admit to a mistake. "*I meant to do that*" is their motto, and they'd do anything to avoid appearing weak or fallible. While that is an extreme example, there are elements of this in most people. We don't like to be wrong, and we don't like to be embarrassed. More ancient human coding.

Considering that, and how protective some become of their manufactured online persona, think of what happens when they post something only to have it be refuted. (We've already covered why pointing out where someone is wrong might only serve to make them cling to the misinformation more tightly.) Many lack the confidence or capacity to say, "*Oh, wow. I did not know that. Thank you for telling me.*" Some can't even stomach quietly backing down or deleting their comment. Instead, out of pride, the misinformation or malformed opinion becomes the hill they will die on.

That person will often seek out like-minded folks, and together they will make one another feel vindicated. (Think of how good it feels when you find someone who understands you or shares your opinion, especially if you felt particularly vulnerable about it.)

And so, some flock this way, some flock that way, the divide grows and intensifies, and many find themselves fighting

Social media not only snatches your time, but it also teaches you attention deficiency.

NEERAJ AGNIHOTRI

an unintentional battle. They might not have felt very convicted about their opinion when they first posted it, but pride and the ancient human code have propelled them directly to the front line, and now they will protect their shaky position at all costs.

Then the other code kicks in. The digital code, shrouded in mystery, continually deciding for them what they'll see based on veiled calculations.

"That algorithm is built around a core mission: promote content that will maximize user engagement," explained *New York Times* columnists Amanda Taub and Max Fisher. "***Posts that tap into negative, primal emotions like anger or fear, studies have found, perform best and so proliferate.***"[12d]

In short, the digital code knows our demons, and the human code insists on defending them.

* * *

The Packaging Problem

Have you ever taken part in a *White Elephant*-style gift exchange? If so, have you ever selected the largest and most attractively wrapped gift, only to find that what was hidden inside wasn't as wonderful (or as large) as the packaging implied? Social media has a similar packaging problem, especially when it comes to news headlines.

The goal is to grab your attention and manipulate emotional triggers that will cause you to click through. You're not going to be interested in or triggered by every bit of news, right? *Wrong.* At least, not if packaging experts have anything to say about it. Tricks of the trade include things like ambiguity, misdirection, overstatement, dramatization, and the ever-popular *missing information*. Consider the following headline....

"Healthy young mother of three dies less than 24 hours after receiving first dose of COVID-19 vaccine."

Many, especially in the early days of COVID-19 vaccinations, would immediately click that headline. Not only do our primitive survival instincts kick in, but it also pulls on emotional levers. But what might have been added to that headline? What could have been missing? What about it might be misleading? What if the truth is that the woman died in a *car accident*, her death was 100% *unrelated* to the vaccine, she was *estranged* from her kids, and *she caused* the accident by driving while intoxicated? Those details do not make the story captivating, so they are summarily omitted.

This is not a stretch, folks. Savvy packagers are exceptionally good at cherry-picking details to lure us in. Pick any mundane or seemingly uninteresting story—they can turn it into juicy, enticing bait in a heartbeat.

* * *

The Propagation Problem

It's bad enough that we allow ourselves to be manipulated by sensationalized headlines and emotional click-bait, which can negatively impact our mental and physical health, but we don't just stop there. We *share* those headlines. We are part of the problem. An excessively big part.

In the same way that laughter is contagious, so are ideas that incite fear or anger. They are more infectious due to our penchant for the negative and our tendency to remember bad memories more distinctly and for longer periods.

I don't mean to suggest that social media invented this issue or is entirely to blame. We've always shared updates by word of mouth, and the sharing of visual news dates back 900 years—to the invention of the printing press. This

Propaganda is a monologue that is not looking for an answer, but an echo.

W.H. AUDEN

allowed us to share information in a new way, including event invitations, the latest gossip, promotional information about a person or group, and, of course, propaganda. Even then, while the goal was to inform, it was also to entice, sell, and distribute.

Social media might not have invented our information issues, but it has taken them to the next level.

The morning after the 2021 Presidential Inauguration, a friend of mine shared a screenshot of their friend's post. This person, who identifies as Liberal, wrote: *"Anyone else starting to realize that they had a codependent relationship with Trump's coverage in the media? I NEED MY HATE-READ TINGLE IN THE MORNING!"* This is a startling admission, but one that many can identify with. Americans who do not agree with whomever the current president is might find humor in the role, openly mock them, or even outright despise them. For the poster above, there was a certain amount of relief that came from connecting with others who felt the same negative feelings for the President as they did, and reading news stories that openly ridiculed him was a form of catharsis. *Misery loves company.* As we struggle with or rejoice in news developments, we find camaraderie on social networks. We confirm a great deal of what we believe based on what others believe, and we justify our behaviors in how others choose to behave.

When we discover a bit of news or gossip that is likely to call forth our like-minded online friends, whether to celebrate it or participate in collective derision, we can't wait to share it. It's like flashing the proverbial "bat signal" to those who share our beliefs and are likely to confirm our feelings.

It's all so codependent.

There are four things we all need to be doing *before* we share information on social media (or anywhere, for that matter).

1. **Read the whole article.** Don't even *think* about passing along something you are not fully aware of.
2. **Fact-check.** Is the information even *true*? Is it fair, balanced, and complete?
3. **Consider the source.** If the content is technically true but the headline is misleading, is there another (better) source for this information? Remember, a staggering number of people *only* read the headline before reacting to or sharing a post. One of the best things you can do is to avoid adding to that problem.
4. **Determine the motive.** Why do you want to share this? Is it useful information? Is it for your benefit or the

benefit of others? What will sharing accomplish? What harm or good could it do?

Bottom line: If you don't have a good reason for sharing something, *don't.* I could continue here, but why bother? It really is as simple as that.

* * *

Here's something to consider about our human coding versus the digital code. Our instinct is to gather information as a means of self-preservation, and the best information is that which is complete, truthful, and unbiased. The algorithm wants to provide us with information that we're likely to interact with and share, and often (currently) that's information that's sensationalized, negative, biased, and contributing to the growing divide. *So, what if we were to hack the code?*

Once we come to understand our ancient instincts and combine that with a rudimentary understanding of how social media algorithms work, we can take steps to counteract that which does not serve us well. Recognizing what we respond to and why is crucial. When we analyze our own biases, triggers, and behaviors, and change our online habits accordingly, the algorithm will learn and change right along with us.

It's not the digital code that is to blame, really. It acts like a mirror, reflecting back at us our inner desires, demons, biases, beliefs, and immoral behavior. *It's up to us to improve the view.*

CHAPTER THIRTEEN

THE ASSENT OF MOB CHARACTER ASSASSINATION

"I believe it's worth thinking about what accountability looks like beyond simply exiling someone. In doing so, we can position ourselves more firmly within the values of social justice."

PRIYANKA PODUGU

Managing Editor, The Brown Daily Herald

I t was Monday, September 5, 1983. The Dallas Cowboys were playing the Washington Redskins, and American sports journalist Howard Cosell was providing commentary. Alvin Garret had just caught yet another pass for a nice gain against the Cowboys when, during the instant replay, Cosell remarked, "Jake Gibbs wanted to get this kid and that little monkey gets loose, doesn't he?"[13a]

Not only did Cosell mistakenly use the wrong name (he meant to say *Joe* Gibbs), but he also used the term "monkey"—which is a very offensive racist term when used to describe someone who is black.

The network received hundreds of calls, and the media response was swift and severe. While some, like sports hero Arthur Ashe, quickly came to Cosell's defense, others—most famously the *Washington Post*—were not so understanding. They called on Cosell to apologize.

Cosell maintained he did not intend for the comment to be derogatory and explained that "monkey" was an affectionate term he used to describe his grandchildren when they ran about quickly in the yard. While that might very well be true, using the term to describe a black man was tone-deaf at best. He completely fumbled his attempted apology and spent weeks in damage control. Even though Alvin Garret issued a statement, "I, Alvin Garrett, think Howard Cosell is just great. And I did not, and do not, take exception to anything he said about me in the broadcast last night. Matter of fact, I am pleased he singled me out for such favorable attention," the backlash continued.[13b]

Cosell's critics wanted more than merely an apology or behavior correction: they were out for blood. They wanted to end his career, and the more they attacked him, the more approval they received from their supporters.

* * *

The term "Cancel Culture" has overtaken the national discussion, but as you can see from the story above, it is not a new phenomenon, nor is it exclusive to any one party or ideology. Those doing the "canceling" have come from both sides of the right-left spectrum. Folks like 49ers quarterback Colin Kaepernick, comedian Bill Maher, and country singers The Dixie Chicks have been effectively *canceled* by the right, while folks like comedian Michael Richards, author J.K. Rowling, and actor Gina Carano felt the wrath from the left.

* * *

Mob Character Assassination

Cancel culture is so much more than merely "falling out of favor" or boycotting. We don't just stop showing up or listening, we want to *burn down the house* on our way out. It could better be described as **mob character assassination**—collectively, purposefully destroying reputation and credibility, and seeking to eliminate power, fame, position, popularity, and platform.

As we have covered, humans are tribalistic, and shaming and shunning (the threat of expulsion) are key components of tribalism. We create societal norms and expectations to protect the integrity of the group and the well-being of its members. *In theory,* there is nothing wrong with applauding pro-social conduct, identifying behaviors that might harm the collective, and eradicating them to create a more inclusive society. In *theory.*

Unlike political character attacks, which are usually deliberate, a mob character assassination is one of opportunity. In the past, most of these "cancelations" were not necessarily divided down party lines (think Michael Jackson or Jimmy "the

Greek" Synder). But as the political rift intensifies, each "side" pursues those on the other like a heat-seeking missile, closing in on targets real, imagined, or fabricated. There is an extra "bonus" layer to it these days, too—in that every time we take someone "out," that's one less player for the opposite team. One fewer soldier on the battlefield.

These mobs employ a mix of open and covert methods to achieve their goals, such as satire, taking comments out of

People get addicted to feeling offended all the time because it gives them a high; being self-righteous and morally superior feels good.

MARK MANSON

context, inflating accusations, nurturing rumors, manipulation, fabrication, exaggeration, or otherwise twisting information. Attacks range in severity from the moderate (admonishing articles, stinging social media posts, parody songs, cartoons, late-night comedy roasting, and negative reviews) to the severe, which might include personally invasive and potentially life-threatening attacks, doxing, residential protests, and threats of violence by phone, email, or in-person (these, sadly, might include threats to a target's family members as well).

One of the strangest and most alarming facets of all this is that each "side" points to the other for launching vicious, unwarranted, and harmful attacks—while summarily denying any wrongdoing on their own "side." This only exacerbates the problem, increasing the buildup of toxic rage and anxiety.

Dictionary definitions of "extremism," such as *the quality or state of being extreme*, do little to help understand the nuances or inherent dangers of extremist behavior. In a 1987 video promoting a UK-based centrist political party, comedian John Cleese said the following,

> *"The biggest advantage of extremism is that it makes you feel good because it provides you with enemies. Let me explain. The remarkable thing about having enemies is that you can pretend that all the badness in the whole world is in your enemies, and all the goodness in the entire world is in you. Attractive, isn't it? If you have a lot of anger and resentment in you anyway, and you, therefore, enjoy abusing people, then you can pretend that you're only doing it because these enemies of yours are such very bad persons and that if it wasn't for them, you'd be good-natured, courteous, and rational all the time. So, if you want to feel good, become an extremist."* [13c]

Being part of a character assassination mob allows people to convince themselves that their worst feelings are virtuous. Rather than recognizing the hostility that resides within them, they can feel that their anger is *evidence* of the righteousness of their cause.

Violent extremism differs from "ordinary" hate or intolerance in that it rationalizes, condones, and encourages drastic measures of a violent nature. It arises from a perception of *us versus them*, intensifies with the conviction that the success of *us* is inseparable from hostile acts against *them*, and culminates with the elimination of the "other side."

***

The Role of Free Speech

Given the scale of our global society, if humans are to coexist we must have mechanisms of accountability. While some of these are innate, others have been ossified into institutions—such as our court system. Without such mechanisms in place, those who feel violated may resort to imposing their own justice, which can trigger the cycle of revenge.

Vengeance and accountability are two vastly different things. Revenge is personal—the goal being to inflict on the perpetrator an amount of suffering comparable to that experienced by the victim. A good mechanism of accountability, on the other hand, is:

- **Established.** *Regulation has been developed, agreed upon, and widely disseminated.*
- **Deliberate.** *Both victim and perpetrator pause to allow for investigation, presentation, discussion, and debate within well-defined processes.*
- **Objective.** *Justice is administered by a neutral third party who is oathbound to adhere to an accepted set of rules.*

Although mechanisms of accountability may be slow, costly, and/or frustrating, without them society would devolve into a dangerous and destructive cycle of revenge.

Reputation is a natural mechanism of accountability, and one that our Founders likely had in mind when they deemed freedom of speech an inalienable right. After all, people are less likely to spread lies if their reputation is at stake. But when the First Amendment was adopted in 1791, who could have imagined that speech would become so decoupled from a person's identity, or that anonymous memes, videos, blogs, tweets, posts, and comments could spread misinformation and disinformation so quickly and so widely?

Today there are hundreds of millions of fake accounts trolling social media, infiltrating comment ecosystems, intentionally disseminating disinformation, and assaulting individuals, businesses, organizations, and governments with little or no liability. The vicious and unrelenting attacks of these anonymous offenders creates a hostile and unsafe environment, and in the absence of meaningful methods of accountability, those who feel violated or vulnerable may enact their own justice.

This is how mob character attacks are born.

I am solidly in favor of eliminating anonymous and unverified accounts on social media. I believe they are responsible for irreparable harm, and their elimination is a

> ##
> *It is imperative that all uprising be guided by an urge for justice, not a craving for revenge.*
>
> ABHIJIT NASKAR

crucial step toward averting societal collapse. While I wholeheartedly believe in the First Amendment and am very wary of regulations on speech, I do believe that our words have consequences and that we must be held responsible for them. Freedom of speech is one of our most sacred rights, but I do not believe it was ever intended to be decoupled from a person's identity or, by extension, the accountability system of reputation.

* * *

Characteristics of Online Mobs

Mob mentality is frightening. When we are part of a large group, we can become less capable of regulating or moderating our behavior. According to *contagion theory*, crowd mindset can have an almost hypnotic effect, and as our mentality becomes part of the collective, we can experience a loss of inhibition and self-awareness, disassociating not only from our actions but from our own identities as well.

There are plenty of things humans will do as part of a group that they would be unlikely to do individually. Within a "mob," behaviors are infectious—and conduct that would normally be objectionable becomes acceptable. The larger the group, the more magnified the behaviors, the greater our sense of anonymity, and the more diminished our sense of responsibility and accountability. Participation can create an adrenaline rush and stir powerful feelings of inclusion. Our need for approval becomes a need for *mob approval*, and we might be willing to violate our moral code to gain it.

Online mobs are remarkably like "real-world" mobs. While there is an absence of immediate physical violence, they can be just as brutal and merciless. There are several key factors, however, that make social media mob character assassinations quite different from normal societal behavior corrections. These include:

Anonymity. Beyond the false sense of anonymity many can experience online, there are actual "fake" (or anonymous) accounts. These profiles may be created by those with a sincere desire for privacy, but often there is a "sniper" behind them— someone who wants to inflict damage on others without facing any risk to their reputation. When an account is not connected to an actual human, or cannot be traced back to a real-world organization, whoever is in control of that account can act with a degree of impunity. They might disassociate themselves from normal moral reasoning, which allows them to do or say the unthinkable.

Bots. Short for "robot," a bot on social media is a fake account that is either fully or partially autonomous and is designed to attract followers, infiltrate pages and groups, automatically post commentary, etc. They are designed to mimic the online behavior of actual humans, making it difficult to "spot the bot." While not all automated accounts are harmful, many are used to disseminate and amplify ideologies and propaganda, or to incite discord. Often, they are used by one "side" to help fuel the cancellation of a rival, or of anyone whose destruction would amount to personal, professional, or political gain. During the 2016 presidential election, bots played a significant role in spreading misinformation. In fact, Twitter identified over 36,000 Russian bots, and the following year Facebook deactivated nearly 700 million fake accounts.[13d]

Unreconciled Revenge. At the core of every mob is a sense that they have been wronged—and sometimes that they deserve revenge. Vengeance tends to be the driving emotion animating mobs.

Humans have a complex and sometimes insatiable desire for vengeance. I've kicked tables while navigating a dark room and momentarily imagined lashing out against inanimate objects void of agency to quest my thirst for retribution. Once, when my 5-year-old son shot me in the eye with a Nerf gun, I was shocked by the sudden flood of aggression I felt. My mind suddenly and momentarily filled with vengeful visions. Obviously, I did not act on any of it, but there it was.

The revenge instinct can feel strangely rewarding. A group of Swiss researchers once scanned the brains of those who had been wronged during an economic exchange game. The subjects had trusted their partners to split a pot of money with them, only to find that their counterparts had chosen to keep the loot for themselves. The subjects were then given a chance to punish their greedy partners, and for a full minute, as the victims contemplated revenge, the activity in their brains was recorded. The decision caused a rush of neural activity in the caudate nucleus, an area of the brain known to

> **"**
>
> *Revenge is the raging fire that consumes the arsonist.*
>
> MAX LUCADO

process *rewards*. The findings gave physiological confirmation to what we've known for years: *revenge is sweet.*[13e]

Or is it? Scientists have discovered many ways in which the practice of revenge fails to fulfill its sweet expectations. Instead of quenching hostility, it may prolong the unpleasantness of the original offense. Further, bringing harm upon an offender is not enough to satisfy a person's vengeful impulses, and may create a cycle of retaliation.

In the real world, if you are harmed by an individual, you seek to right the wrong and move on. *In the digital realm, as battles rage between nebulous and fractious groups, an individual might never feel reconciled—only increasingly emboldened for more vicious attacks.*

* * *

The Cyclone

While shaming and shunning are ancient tactics, assaults and impacts are drastically amplified and reproduced in modern times. This is due to a blend of technology and sensationalism I call *The Cyclone*.

Ancient humans might have shamed one another—they might even have inspired others to do the same. But once the shaming had been carried out, the incident concluded, and life moved on. Not so with The Cyclone, which is a phenomenon unique to our time. The Cyclone not only inspires and drives shaming and shunning, but it also replicates and perpetuates it in alarming ways. This is due to several factors, including:

- **Partisan Division.** *In decades past, there were liberal Republicans and conservative Democrats, but now each party is "purer," and it's much more likely that people of one party do not know people of the other. When we don't have human experiences providing us with nuanced empathetic connections—and when we rely on the extreme hyperbolic caricatures created by the media—it creates intense "othering," putting us on the defensive, ready to fight at the drop of a hat.*

- **Unmoderated Social Media.** *Our entrenched value of freedom of speech, combined with online anonymity, has created a toxic environment of people descending into uncivil conversations and personal attacks. Much of social media has become a cesspool of sensationalism, misinformation, and personal assaults, and the anonymity factor only adds to the problem.*

A lie can travel halfway around the world while the truth is putting on its shoes.

UNKNOWN

- **Hyper Reinforcement.** *Breaches in social norms are reported at breathtaking speed via multiple avenues— including television, radio, internet, and social media—then* *reinforced before due diligence or moral reasoning can occur. Information is shot out; judgments are made and supported by a hive mind. Facts and fictions are introduced and reinforced so quickly that our brains cannot discern between hearsay and firsthand witnessing.*

The Cyclone is what happens when you add algorithmically driven technology to the characteristics of mob mentality, fierce partisan divides, and asymmetric reinforcement.

THE CYCLONE PROCESS

Story Broadcast

Bird on a Wire Phenomenon

The Algorithm

Mob Extremism

Bots Amplify

Story Broadcast
Television, print, social media, etc.

Bird on a Wire Phenomenon
Editors, producers, and influencers behave like a "bird on a wire"—erupting from their place to follow the flock. The mass creates its own "mind," where each bird zigs and zags to maintain the safety and momentum of the flock.

The Algorithm
Social media algorithms sense the opportunity to hook "users" on outrage by promoting posts about the story to the top of feeds. The algorithm inherent in all technology turbo charges everything. The algorithm is the mathematical equivalent of a digital sociopath whose singular goal is to maintain your attention, regardless of the cost to you or to society.

Bots Amplify
Fake social media accounts devoted to disunity (and often controlled by other countries) seize the opportunity to divide and distract Americans by liking, commenting, sharing, and creating even more exaggerated "stories"—injecting gasoline into the raging fire. Americans fighting Americans is the greatest gift to our adversaries.

Mob Extremism

Gaining faux notoriety by identifying the "wrongdoing," members also gain satisfaction. The "cheater detection mechanism" is enacted by other members who join in the fight. Oxytocin and adrenaline flow as members feel the power of inclusion and extremism. Bolstered by mob mentality and a sense of anonymity, all nuance and reason are lost. The language, aggressive threats, and tactics become extreme. Each member tries to "one-up" the others with more vicious attacks.

* * *

The End of Understanding

If a friend made a racist, intolerant, or insensitive remark, what would your primary goal or hope for them be?

A. *To help them understand and acknowledge their error, apologize, and make steps towards improvement.*

B. *To ensure they never earn a living again.*

C. *To eradicate them from the planet.*

Most of us (and I hope you) would choose option A and never even consider options B or C. Everyone makes mistakes, and we've all said something insensitive at some point. We would not be at all interested in getting even with that friend or seeking revenge. Because while shunning is a valid tool in our ancient corrective toolbox, we recognize that it should only be used for those people who cannot be rehabilitated or who present a clear and present danger to ourselves or our community.

When we participate in mob character assassination, however, we respond very differently. As the target is not a friend, we are instantly less understanding and sympathetic. There are no second chances. Like a real-world mob, when a character assassination mob forms they lose perspective, nuance, and reasoning ability. We are out for blood, and no apology or correction will suffice. Complete annihilation becomes the only viable solution.

> **"**
>
> *It's an oversimplification of somebody's worth to 'cancel' them.*
>
> HARI NEFF

* * *

The
Backfire Effect

Many arrogantly and foolishly believe that they (either individually or collectively) will be able to "cancel" someone quickly and cleanly, especially if there are large numbers on their side. This is rarely the case. Think back to "The Pride Problem"—the louder one cries foul, the deeper the other might dig in their heels. We also have a noticeably large "Oh yeah? Well, what about *you?*" problem in this country. Whether online, in politics, or even interpersonally, when a finger is pointed at us we tend to point one right back.

This leads to a new problem, canceling the canceler—simultaneously bashing and embracing their mob tactics. Now each side is capitalizing on what the other side is canceling. They blame one another for being unreasonable, reckless, and idiotic, and they conclude that complaints from the other side amount to nothing more than childish foot-stamping. That, of course, infuriates the "other" side, and the cycle continues.

* * *

#Options

In interpersonal relationships, there are several corrective measures we can employ to deal with an offense. When someone says or does something offensive, here are some options to consider (in ascending order):

- Ask them to stop.
- Share with them why what they are doing is inappropriate, and ask them to stop.
- Share with them why what they are doing is inappropriate, ask them to stop, and request an apology.
- Distance yourself from that person.

- Without getting personal, share your concerns with others.*
- If you feel threatened and cannot safely remove yourself, call for assistance or law enforcement.

* *But isn't this gossip? Yes, but it's important to realize that not all gossip is inherently "bad." When used properly, it can unify, deepen intimacy across large groups, and build cohesion.*

CHAPTER FOURTEEN

BETTER SAFE THAN SORRY?

"Conspiracy theorists don't need facts. They have their imaginations. They can invent their own."

RON ELVING

Senior Editor and Correspondent, NPR

H ave you ever fallen for a conspiracy theory? Before you answer that, let me make this clear—believing in a conspiracy theory is not a behavior reserved for the unintelligent. On the contrary, there are sound evolutionary reasons why we tend to accept them.

In our ancient past, when tribal feuds existed, it would be helpful to be able to spot a conspirator. It might be the difference between life and death, for you and your tribal community. Fast forward to today. If you hear a rustling behind you, and I tell you to move because there's a giant, deadly spider about to pounce on you, what's the safer choice? To believe me, or to stay put?

People accept conspiracy theories because—instinctually— it feels like the safe thing to do. We think, *better safe than sorry!* Our brains are wired to accept them, and there's a chance you believe in some right now without even knowing it. Research has found that half of the country believes in at least one.[14a]

If I were to put two plastic balls in a bag, one red and one blue, then blindfold you and ask you to pick one out of the bag— and if you chose the red ball four times in a row—what do you think would happen on the fifth pull? If you are thinking the next pull would *have* to be blue because five reds in a row would be so unlikely, that is due to a cognitive bias known as *Illusory Pattern Perception*. It's a bias that causes us to try to "connect the dots," so to speak. To create order where there is chaos by identifying patterns in random stimuli.

If you were thinking, however, *"Well, there's always a 50/50 chance, so it could be red or blue,"* that is technically correct. Mathematically, there is always a 50% chance you would draw either color. What you drew the previous four times has nothing to do with the fifth pull.

Those who were influenced by the perceived pattern of red pulls could be more likely to accept conspiracy theories, and once one of these theories takes root, confirmation bias can make our belief in them even stronger.

Conspiracy theories create division. Much like political convictions, people can become so engrossed in them that they perceive those who do *not* believe them as being their enemy. So how can we identify conspiracy theories and thus better avoid falling victim to them?

- **Look at the numbers.** *One of the first things I like to consider is—how many people would have to be collectively keeping this a secret? The larger that number is, the less likely it's possible. The same goes for the size of the ambition behind the theory, and the amount of power that would be required to pull it off. Again, the bigger either of those is, the smaller the likelihood that any of it is true.*

- **Consider the source.** *Who is floating this theory? Is this someone who seems otherwise intelligent, trustworthy, and respected? Or is it someone who has a history of being suspicious, contrary, or anti-establishment?*

- **Gauge complexity.** *How many elements are there to this theory? How intricate is the web, how loose are the connections, and how many different things would all have to be true and working in cahoots for this to be real?*

- **Weigh the evidence.** *Is it well researched, and from reputable sources? Or is it mostly speculative assumptions?*

- **How are facts treated?** *If verified, proven evidence to the contrary is summarily ignored or discarded, that's a big sign that things don't add up.*

So, what can you do if someone you know has been sucked into what you're certain is a conspiracy theory? Attempting to refute or debunk it is unlikely to go well (and could very well backfire). The best suggestion I can give is that you engage in an open conversation—one in which you listen more than speak. Ask how they have reached their conclusions, and be empathetic, not dismissive. Remember that they think of themselves as healthy skeptics, and they think that their theories have been well researched (even though that "research" may be fueled by confirmation bias). Do your best to make them feel safe and heard, and give them a sense of belonging. You might not get far, but it's worth the effort, and a thoughtful dialogue can be a powerful thing.

CHAPTER FIFTEEN

IS SOCIAL MEDIA TURNING YOU INTO AN EXTREMIST?

"What is objectionable, what is dangerous about extremists is not that they are extreme, but that they are intolerant. The evil is not what they say about their cause, but what they say about their opponents."

ROBERT F. KENNEDY

Former U.S. Attorney General and Politician

A s I write these words, there is a rising tide of extremist movements in the United States, and it is threatening to destabilize our country. It would be simple to see extremists as "them," but could it be that *they* are *us*?

Americans have become particularly good at identifying extremism in "other" groups, both in and outside of the United States. However, extremists often cannot recognize it within themselves. Even if they do, they tend to excuse any objectionable behavior or violent means because they feel their actions are justified. Social media is giving rise to new legions of extremists from all walks of life due to the following....

- **Anonymity**
  You can harbor racist, hateful ideology with negligible risk to your reputation if you are hiding behind a fake or obscured online profile.

- **Ease of Assembly**
  Before the advent of social media, there was much more organization involved, and extremists had to plan actual real-world meetings. They had to find public venues willing to host public gatherings to share hateful ideologies and gain supporters. Your local "Starbucks" isn't too excited about having a "Racists Unite Rally" at their store.

- **Speedy Reinforcements**
  Typically, for propaganda to grab hold and take seed, it must be seen and/or heard repeatedly. Hundreds of years ago this took more time. It could be days or even weeks between visual or verbal reinforcements of fallacious propaganda. Now one can see the same disinformation or indoctrination dozens of times in a single minute.

* * *

Deconstruction of an Extremist

Laird Wilcox founded the Wilcox Collection on Contemporary Political Movements in the Kenneth Spencer Library at the University of Kansas in 1965. As a prominent researcher on political groups, he has written numerous books, essays, and reports on the radicalization of all types of groups and organizations. Wilcox published *The Hoaxer Project Report: Racist and Anti-Semitic Graffiti, Harassment and Violence: An Essay on Hoaxes and Fabricated Incidents* in which he included twenty-one traits of extremism.[15a] He has graciously permitted me to reprint his list, in full, here. (*Thank you, again, Laird!*) As you read this, bear in mind that it was first published in 1990.

21 EXTREMIST TRAITS
By Laird Wilcox

1. CHARACTER ASSASSINATION. Extremists often attack the character of an opponent rather than deal with the facts or issues raised. They will question motives, qualifications, past associations, alleged values, personality, looks, mental health, and so on as a diversion from the issues under consideration. Some of these matters are not entirely irrelevant, but they should not serve to avoid the genuine issues. Extremists object strenuously when this is done to them, of course.

2. NAME-CALLING AND LABELING. Extremists are quick to resort to epithets (racist, subversive, pervert, hate monger, nut, crackpot, degenerate, un-American, anti-Semite, red, Commie, Nazi, kook, fink, liar, bigot, and so on) to label and condemn opponents to divert attention from their arguments and to discourage others from hearing them out. These epithets do not have to be proved to be effective; the mere fact that they have been said is often enough.

3. **IRRESPONSIBLE SWEEPING GENERALIZATIONS.** Extremists tend to make sweeping claims or judgments on little or no evidence, and they tend to confuse similarity with sameness. That is, they assume that because two (or more) things, events, or persons are alike in some respects, they must be alike in most respects. The sloppy use of analogy is a treacherous form of logic and has a high potential for false conclusions.

4. **INADEQUATE PROOF FOR ASSERTIONS.** Extremists tend to be very fuzzy about what constitutes proof, and they also tend to get caught up in logical fallacies, such as post hoc ergo propter hoc (if a prior event explains a subsequent occurrence simply because of their before and after relationship). They tend to project wished-for conclusions and exaggerate the significance of the information that confirms their beliefs while derogating or ignoring information that contradicts them. They tend to be motivated by feelings more than facts, by what they want to exist rather than what does exist. Extremists do a lot of wishful and fearful thinking.

5. **ADVOCACY OF DOUBLE STANDARDS.** Extremists tend to judge themselves or their interest group in terms of their intentions, which they tend to view very generously, and others by their acts, which they tend to view very critically. They would like you to accept their assertions on faith, but they demand proof for yours. They tend to engage in special pleading* on behalf of themselves or their interests, usually because of some alleged special status, past circumstances, or present disadvantage.

6. **TENDENCY TO VIEW THEIR OPPONENTS AND CRITICS AS ESSENTIALLY EVIL.** To the extremist, opponents hold opposing positions because they are bad people, immoral, dishonest, unscrupulous, mean-spirited, hateful, cruel, or whatever, not merely because they simply disagree, see the matter differently, have competing interests, or are even mistaken.

7. MANICHAEAN WORLDVIEW. Extremists tend to see the world in terms of absolutes of good and evil, for them or against them, with no middle ground or intermediate positions. All issues are moral issues of right and wrong, with the "right" position coinciding with their interests. Their slogan is often "those who are not with me are against me."

8. ADVOCACY OF SOME DEGREE OF CENSORSHIP OR REPRESSION OF THEIR OPPONENTS AND/OR CRITICS. This may include a highly active campaign to keep opponents from media access and a public hearing, as in the case of blacklisting, banning, or "quarantining" dissident spokespersons. They may lobby for legislation against speaking, writing, teaching, or instructing "subversive" or forbidden information or opinions. They may even attempt to keep offending books out of stores or off library shelves, discourage advertising with threats of reprisals, and keep spokespersons for "offensive" views off the airwaves or certain columnists out of newspapers. In each case, the goal is information control. Extremists would prefer that you listen only to them. They feel threatened when someone talks back or challenges their views.

9. TEND TO IDENTIFY THEMSELVES IN TERMS OF WHO THEIR ENEMIES ARE: WHOM THEY HATE AND WHO HATES THEM. Accordingly, extremists may become emotionally bound to their opponents, who are often competing extremists themselves. Because they tend to view their enemies as evil and powerful, they tend, subconsciously, to emulate them, adopting the same tactics. For example, anti-Communist and anti-Nazi groups often behave surprisingly like their opponents. Anti-Klan rallies often take on much of the character of the stereotype of Klan rallies themselves, including the orgy of emotion, bullying, screaming epithets, and even acts of violence. To behave the opposite of someone is to surrender your will to them, and "opposites" are often more like mirror images that, although they have "left" and "right" reversed, look, and behave amazingly alike.

10. TENDENCY TOWARD ARGUMENT BY INTIMIDATION. Extremists tend to frame their arguments in such a way as to intimidate others into accepting their premises and conclusions. To disagree with them is to "ally oneself with the devil," or to give aid and comfort to the enemy. They use a lot of moralizing and pontificating and tend to be very judgmental. This shrill, harsh rhetorical style allows them to keep their opponents and critics on the defensive, cuts off troublesome lines of argument, and allows them to define the perimeters of debate.

11. USE OF SLOGANS, BUZZWORDS, AND THOUGHT-STOPPING CLICHES. For many extremists' shortcuts in thinking and in reasoning matters out seem to be necessary to avoid or evade awareness of troublesome facts and compelling counterarguments. Extremists behave in ways that reinforce their prejudices and alter their own consciousness in a manner that bolsters their false confidence and sense of self-righteousness.

12. ASSUMPTION OF MORAL OR OTHER SUPERIORITY OVER OTHERS. Most claims of general racial or ethnic superiority—a master race, for example. Less obvious are claims of ennoblement because of alleged victimhood, a special relationship with God, membership in a special "elite" or "class," and an aloof "high-minded" snobbishness that accrues because of the weightiness of their preoccupations, their altruism, and their willingness to sacrifice themselves (and others) to their cause. Who can bear to deal with common people when one is trying to save the world! Extremists can show great indignation when one is "insensitive" enough to challenge these claims.

13. DOOMSDAY THINKING. Extremists often predict dire or catastrophic consequences from a situation or from failure to follow a specific course, and they tend to exhibit a kind of "crisis-mindedness." It can be a Communist takeover, a Nazi revival, nuclear war, earthquakes, floods, or the wrath of God. Whatever it is, it's just around the corner unless we follow their program and listen to the special insight and wisdom, to which only the truly enlightened have access. For extremists, any setback or defeat is the "beginning of the end!"

14. BELIEF THAT IT'S OKAY TO DO BAD THINGS IN THE SERVICE OF A "GOOD" CAUSE. Extremists may deliberately lie, distort, misquote, slander, defame, or libel their opponents and critics, engage in censorship or repression, or undertake violence in "special cases." This is done with little or no remorse if it's in the service of defeating the Communists or Fascists or whomever. Defeating an "enemy" becomes an all-encompassing goal to which other values are subordinate. With extremists, the end justifies the means.

15. EMPHASIS ON EMOTIONAL RESPONSES AND, CORRESPONDINGLY, LESS IMPORTANCE ATTACHED TO REASONING AND LOGICAL ANALYSIS. Extremists have an unspoken reverence for propaganda, which they may call "education" or "consciousness-raising." Symbolism plays an exaggerated role in their thinking, and they tend to think imprecisely and metamorphically. Harold D. Lasswell, in his book, *Psychopathology and Politics*, says, "The essential mark of the agitator is the high value he places on the emotional response of the public." Effective extremists tend to be effective propagandists. Propaganda differs from education in that the former teaches one what to think, and the latter teaches one how to think.

16. HYPERSENSITIVITY AND VIGILANCE. Extremists perceive hostile innuendo in even casual comments; imagine rejection and antagonism concealed in honest disagreement and dissent; see "latent" subversion, anti-Semitism, perversion, racism, disloyalty, and so on in innocent gestures and ambiguous behaviors. Although few extremists are clinically paranoid, many of them adopt a paranoid style with its attendant hostility and distrust.

17. USE OF SUPERNATURAL RATIONALE FOR BELIEFS AND ACTIONS. Some extremists, particularly those involved in "cults" or extreme religious movements, such as fundamentalist Christians, militant Zionist extremists, and members of mystical and metaphysical organizations, claim supernatural rationale for their beliefs and actions, and that their movement or cause is ordained by God. In this case, stark extremism may become reframed in a "religious" context, which can have a legitimizing effect for some people. It's surprising how many people are reluctant to challenge religiously motivated extremism because it represents "religious belief" or because of the sacred-cow status of some religions in our culture.

18. PROBLEMS TOLERATING AMBIGUITY AND UNCERTAINTY. Indeed, the ideologies and belief systems to which extremists tend to attach themselves often represent grasping for certainty in an uncertain world, or an attempt to achieve absolute security in an environment that is naturally unpredictable or populated by people with interests opposed to their own. Extremists exhibit a kind of risk-aversiveness that compels them to engage in controlling and manipulative behavior, both on a personal level and in a political context, to protect themselves from the unforeseen and unknown. The more laws or "rules" there are that regulate the behavior of others – particularly their "enemies"–the more secure extremists feel.

19. INCLINATION TOWARD "GROUPTHINK." Extremists, their organizations, and their subcultures are prone to an inward-looking group cohesiveness that leads to what Irving Janis discussed in his excellent book Victims of Groupthink. "Groupthink" involves a tendency to conform to group norms and to preserve solidarity and concurrence at the expense of distorting members' observations of facts, conflicting evidence, and disquieting observations that would call into question the shared assumptions and beliefs of the group.

Extremists, for example, talk only with one another, read material that reflects their own views, and can be almost phobic about the "propaganda" of the "other side." The result is a deterioration of reality-testing, rationality, and moral judgment. With groupthink, shared illusions of righteousness, superior morality, persecution, and so on remain intact, and those who challenge them are viewed with skepticism and hostility.

20. TENDENCY TO PERSONALIZE HOSTILITY. Extremists often wish for the personal bad fortune of their "enemies," and celebrate when it occurs. When a critic or an adversary dies or has a serious illness, a bad accident, or personal legal problems, extremists often rejoice and chortle about how they "deserved" it. I recall seeing right-wing extremists celebrate the assassination of Martin Luther King and leftists agonizing because George Wallace survived an assassination attempt. In each instance, their hatred was not only directed against ideas, but also against individual human beings.

21. EXTREMISTS OFTEN FEEL THAT THE SYSTEM IS NO GOOD UNLESS THEY WIN. For example, if they lose an election, then it was "rigged." If public opinion turns against them, it was because of "brainwashing." If their followers become disillusioned, it's because of "sabotage." The test of the rightness or wrongness of the system is how it impacts them.

---

* Special pleading is an argument in which the speaker deliberately ignores aspects that are unfavorable to their point of view.

CHAPTER SIXTEEN

WHO'S ON THE OTHER SIDE OF THE COMMENTS?

"Hatred and fear blind us.
We no longer see each other.
We only see the faces of monsters,
and that gives us the courage
to destroy each other."

THICH NHAT HANH
Zen Master, Vietnamese Thiền Buddhist Monk

Y ou're hurrying down the road, the highway clear and wide ahead of you, and the sun is shining at the perfect angle as you drive. You're excited to reach your destination and see nothing that might slow you down.

A car inches up on your left side, and you're prepared to let them pass. But when you look ahead to an upcoming on-ramp, you see several cars about to merge with your lane. You know you need to slow down or switch lanes, but with the ramp quickly approaching, you decide moving left is best.

Because the car beside you was trying to pass, you end up cutting them off. Clearly, this upsets them, and they proceed to blare their horn at you. Once the new arrivals have merged onto the highway, you switch back to the right lane and offer a sheepish wave as the car on the left speeds by.

You reach your exit, turn down the street of your destination, and find that it is packed with cars. You come to a stop at a red light, several cars back, and wait for it to turn green. When it finally does, the car at the front of the pack doesn't move right away, and you sigh in exasperation. Eventually, that car does move, and while most of the vehicles in front of you make it through the light, it turns red before you and the car in front of you can proceed through the intersection. You wait through another light cycle and finally your light is green again, but the car in front of you doesn't move. You tap your horn, yell *"Come on!"*, then honk two more times. The car in front of you turns, and you're able to reach your destination.

* * *

Road Rage

Expressions of road rage while behind the wheel are not altogether unlike manifestations of rage while on social media, due to the level of anonymity or safety we feel "behind" a keyboard. In the case of road rage, we forget any connection to our fellow driver and instead direct all our anger or frustration toward the physical vehicle ours is "interacting" with. Think about it—the last time you were angered on the highway, who did it? Do you remember a person or a maroon SUV? You remember the vehicle. And while that is quite common, separating driver from vehicle is an act of *dehumanization* and *objectification.*

In this example, we are disregarding the humanity of the driver, their emotions and reactions, and refusing to allow for human error. As for objectification, we are expressing our rage toward a vehicle with tactics we would (hopefully) never use when face-to-face with a fellow human being. Think about the same scenario, but you and the other driver are operating motorcycles and can see one another's faces clearly. Would that change anything? *You bet it would.*

* * *

Post Rage

The rage behaviors we exhibit while behind the wheel aren't healthy, but they're unlikely to trigger a civil war. Unfortunately, the same cannot be said for the rage we express on social media.

After reading a story on Reddit, for example, it would be easy enough for the user to scroll on to the next story; however, interaction via the comments section is part of the platform's culture—practically a required form of participation. As a result, Redditors comment with abandon, often being brutally honest, harsh, and overly critical. This can make the platform feel unsafe for more empathetic readers. They might elect to deactivate their accounts or ignore the comments section over time.

Though Reddit's structure provides a prime example of the implied importance of a comments section, it certainly does not stand alone. Commenting on posts and tweets on other popular platforms, such as Facebook or Twitter, is part of the "culture" of those spaces as well. Arguments break out over political posts daily, and the comments section is often filled with more than counter-arguments—criticisms, personal jabs, and even bullying tactics and threats are commonplace.

He who takes offense when no offense is intended is a fool, and he who takes offense when offense is intended is a greater fool.

BRIGHAM YOUNG

When a person from one "side" provides a particularly stinging retort, those on the other "side" jump in to do battle, ganging up against them. Often the responses become so aggressive and excessive that threads into the hundreds of comments can develop in a matter of minutes.

"Don't hang out in the comments section" is a popular, well-known piece of advice these days—and for good reason. It is impossible to say with certainty where the advice originated, but it was in response to comment threads that accompanied YouTube videos. On this platform, viewers being able to use creative usernames (rather than legal names) allowed them to post with a greater degree of anonymity. Rude, hurtful, even hateful comments resulted in minimal accountability. No one was spared. It got so bad that YouTube now automatically turns off commenting if a video features children.[16a]

On a platform like Facebook, where there has been a recent push to use only legal names, commenting can be slightly less harsh—but only slightly. We still cannot seem to stop ourselves from posting a barrage of comments, often when we feel the need to be "right" or teach someone else something. This is another example of an *evolutionary mismatch*, in which we engage with someone as an attempt at social betterment. Somehow, we manage to believe that if we show them the error of their ways, they will improve on the spot, and our society will be all the better for it.

This tactic might have worked in ancient times, when a correction could have been adjusting someone's hunting or foraging technique to impact the tribe quickly and positively, but a person's social behaviors in the modern day are not so easily corrected. Instead of creating a "lightbulb moment" for someone, in which they realize they have been wrong all along, we are more likely to create feelings of anger, resentment, or embarrassment. Even if we were "only trying to help," it is probable the other party will not see it that way. It is more likely to be read as judgment, belittlement, and arrogance.

* * *

Persistence is Futile

Political posts are less about trying to inform or even influence others, and more like raising a flag to ask *who's with me and who's against me?* Those who "like" and positively comment are our "brothers in arms," and those who "dislike" or voice disagreement become the enemy—and reinforce just how "right" we feel in our convictions. We use this information to know who is "dumb" or "wrong," versus who we can commiserate with about them.

I used to post about politics until I understood the utter futility. *Social media posts of a political nature do not—both for cultural and technological reasons—stimulate healthy civic discourse, engender empathy or understanding, or serve to share knowledge in a meaningful way.*

In fact, political posts often have the opposite effect of what the original poster expected or intended.

Think of it this way: religious missionaries often walk hundreds of miles and knock on thousands of doors before someone even lets them inside (let alone converts to their faith). Many face more than slammed doors, enduring insults or even threats of physical harm. But does this deter them from their mission? Quite the reverse. After an emotionally challenging day full of rejection, they return to their homes and commiserate with their fellow missionaries. They find solace, comfort, and solidarity in the painful experience—and it only deepens their indoctrination and devotion to their faith.

Every time you argue with someone online, you are providing them with emotional leverage to further retreat and entrench themselves in their own (misguided) ideology. The best way to create a dogmatic enemy is to argue with them. The more you fight them, the more entrenched their wretched ideological cancer becomes.

Impersonal Inflammation

Part of the problem is the impersonal nature of online interactions. When you attempt to change lanes while driving, if another driver is in your blind spot they'll honk. This is technically a helpful gesture for both cars, in that it helps to ensure that an accident does not occur. But if we become aggressive in our honking, the other party can feel highly affronted. The same is true of the comments section on social media. We can become too aggressive, eschewing empathy and kindness in favor of correctness—often resorting to judgment, shaming, or condemnation.

If we're honest with ourselves, it's especially easy to turn a comments section into an unsafe space when someone of another political party is involved. If you're already feeling intolerant of, say, liberals, and a liberal makes a comment you do not agree with, hiding behind a keyboard (and even an anonymous username) might be all you need to resort to open ridicule. In your mind, they have already become a sort of "other," and when you're interacting with text on a screen, rather than face-to-face with

Every social association that is not face-to-face is injurious to your health.

NASSIM NICHOLAS TALEB

an actual person, it becomes even easier to objectify the person and their motives.

Picture someone who has already established an opinion of another person's political party, developed a stereotypical caricature of "them" in their mind, and witnessed others posting content that confirms those biases. They might be utilizing social media on *high alert,* waiting for the "other" to lash out in some way—further confirming what they think they know about "them." They might even be, on some level, anxious to see it. They've built up ammunition for an attack—in the form of at-the-ready insults, evidence, and criticisms—and are continually lying in wait for an "other" to fire the first shot. When that confirmative evidence does appear, they unload all their ammunition before the "other" has a chance to reload (or even realize what is happening).

Commenting, in and of itself, is not the problem. The ability to respond to a post doesn't *create* hostility, and there are certainly many worthwhile, constructive, kind contributions that can be made on social media. It's all a matter of what we post, how we comment, and how we respond to those comments—not to mention how *impulsively* we do any of those things. If we could learn to modify our use of and engagement on these platforms, time spent on social media could be a much more mindful, empathetic, beneficial, and rewarding experience.

CHAPTER SEVENTEEN

RAGE AGAINST THE OUTRAGE MACHINE

"Do not bite at the bait of pleasure till you know there is no hook beneath it."

THOMAS JEFFERSON

United States Founding Father and 3rd President

G iven the fact that our phones are instant-gratification machines, it's no wonder that so many of us struggle with excessive daily use. But if we hope to improve, individually and collectively, we're going to have to work through that addiction, sever our unhealthy attachment to them, and stop the dehumanization and demonization of our fellow citizens.

Six months ago, I was on the phone with my friend, Zack. We were talking about politics, sharing our concerns for the country, and having what I thought was a meaningful conversation when suddenly he said something profoundly disturbing. He mentioned the number of Americans who supported one particular President and said "*Honestly? If I could put a gun to each of their heads, and blow them off, I would.*"

I was shocked.

This was the moment I realized that our country's division had grown far beyond what I had feared. I realized what we were doing wasn't working. What *I* was doing wasn't working. Blaming others for the political climate, arguing with them online, calling up friends like Zack to complain about politics— none of it was working. *At that moment, I decided I wanted to do something about it. I had to find a way to make a difference.*

A few days later, I called Zack again. He had told me, at one point, that he normally spent several hours per day on social networks, so he wanted to talk about *keyboard warrioring*—the illusion that one is making a difference through their use of social media, when in fact they might be only perpetuating the problem. I also wanted to bring up *the backfire effect*, which leads people to dig their heels in deeper when someone challenges their beliefs. And I wanted to challenge him to change his behavior. Social media had become a significant problem for him, and I was going to encourage him to discontinue his relationship with it entirely. I approached it very carefully, cautiously, and without judgment.

There's a longer story here, but the condensed version is that while it was not immediate or pain-free, Zack managed to significantly alter his online behavior, forgoing the 3 to 4 hours per day he used to spend on social media. He also went on a complete news blackout for 90 days. During that time, I interviewed his wife, Emma, who said that Zack had become a vastly different person. He was no longer ranting, raging, or screaming at the television, and Emma noted the following:

- *He slept more.*
- *He was in a good mood most of the time.*
- *He was much more interesting.*
- *They got out to see friends more, and there was no arguing when they did so.*
- *He was decisively "present," and they were able to share stories about their lives, connect, and engage in meaningful, empathetic conversations.*

Finally, she told me, *"I feel as though I not only have my husband back but my life back."*

Zack's story is a fitting example of how changing our relationship with social media can have a positive impact not only on our own lives but on those around us as well. I challenge *you* to take a hard look at your current online behaviors and determine where changes might be in order. *(If the idea of cutting back on social networking makes you uncomfortable, that's an almost sure sign that you need to make some significant adjustments.)*

* * *

WHAT DO YOU NEED IN YOUR POCKET (REALLY)?

You don't require social media at your fingertips every moment of the day, most of us do not need 24/7/365 access to email either, and the vast majority of people on your contact list do *not* need to be able to reach you at any hour.

Once you take this in, realize it's true, and believe it for yourself, *you are in control.* YOU can decide what you really need to carry with you, versus what can stay at your desk. Removing social media apps from your phone could eliminate a great deal of "noise" from your life; and while some apps, such as Instagram or TikTok, are adapted specifically for smartphones, you can still access them from a computer.

Imagine going throughout your day, completing your tasks, interacting with people, and enjoying nature . . . without a constant pinging in your pocket as new notifications roll in.

You can also adjust the notifications on your phone, including what sounds you will use (if any) and whether or not to use the vibrate feature (which has been shown to cause increased anxiety response in some mobile users).[17a] You can set specific times at which you can or cannot be reached, and adapt your contact list—so that important contacts (such as children) can reach you at any time, but others will be diverted to voice mail if they call during one of the pre-determined periods that you've decided to be "unavailable." *(I considered listing instructions here, but since phones and their settings change so often, the best idea is to search online for instructions that are specific to your phone type, model, and operating system.)*

* * *

TREAT YOUR PHONE LIKE A TOOTHBRUSH

When we think of a tool like a toothbrush, we think of necessity. When our teeth need to be cleaned, and at regularly scheduled intervals, we pick up the brush and utilize it. When finished, it has served its purpose, and the tool is put away.

The best tools we have at our disposal work like the toothbrush. They are simple, in that they help us to complete the task we need to perform with only a small amount of our attention and while taking the minimum amount of time from our lives. By this measure, our phones are terrible, over-equipped tools. They still have calling and texting features, and it's convenient to be able to search for something at the drop of a hat, but all of the added capabilities and features tend to distract us more often than they assist us. Have you ever picked up your phone to text a question to a loved one only to get pulled into a social media conversation, or a game, or your email—leaving you to question later why you picked up your phone in the first place? This is the problem in a nutshell. We should be in control of the tool, not the other way around.

The solution? *We must start treating our phones like the tools they are and were meant to be.*

There's no denying that having your phone available in an emergency is important (thinking back, this was the reason many people purchased their first cellular phone). So, take it with you when you leave the house if you feel you need it. But limit your use and adjust your notification and availability settings to minimize

Kill your notifications. Yes, really. Turn them all off. You'll discover that you don't miss the stream of cards filling your lockscreen, because they never existed for your benefit.

DAVID PIERCE

distractions. At home, try leaving it in a room that you aren't in throughout the day, such as your bedroom. Place it on the nightstand and go about your day in the living room, kitchen, and other spaces.

The typical American brushes their teeth in the morning, in the evening, and if/as needed throughout the day. Consider adopting a similar schedule for your phone. Check in, in the morning, to address any important tasks early in the day, then set it aside until an hour or so before bed, retrieving it only if necessary. Spend no more than 30 minutes catching up on what you felt you "missed" throughout the day, and then leave your screen behind about 30 minutes before lying down to sleep. This will allow your brain to rest and relax, and it might improve your sleep.

* * *

SCROLL LESS, READ MORE

According to Facebook's global creative director, Andrew Keller, "*The average person scrolls through 300 feet, or one Statue of Liberty, of mobile content every day.*" That's over 20 miles per year! And how much time do we spend social networking? 145 minutes (about 2 and a half hours) per day, which adds up to just under 37 days per year. Read that again. We're spending more than a month each year on social media. *That's insane.*[17b]

It's quite possible to curb our screen usage while remaining well-informed and entertained. The most straight-forward way is to *read more*.

Many people point to reading as one of their favorite pastimes, and others look back on the hours they spent relaxing with a delightful book in fond nostalgia. The trouble is, many have convinced themselves that they simply don't have the time to read "these days." Ironically, here are a few things they *do* have time for: texting, scrolling through social media, Netflix binges, etc.

Thinking back to Zack, he gained about 3-4 hours per day (21-28 hours per week) when he curbed his social media habit. Reducing the amount of time you devote to your social media habit could be a massive win-win—not only do you improve your overall health and well-being, but you might also finally have the time to read!

I'm not suggesting that we stop texting or checking social media altogether, but trading some of the time we're mindlessly scrolling through our phones for reading real, physical books would be wildly beneficial. The same goes for our use of Netflix and other streaming services. While it's admittedly good for our minds to track a story, and of course enjoyable, filmed entertainment is screen-based, and there are adverse effects to prolonged screen time.

It all goes back to brain health: the more stress you place on your brain, the more gray matter is depleted, which impacts your ability to reason, make decisions, and empathize. It also leads to a rise in physical ailments, such as headaches, high blood pressure, insomnia, depression, anxiety, and decreased emotional regulation, particularly regarding anger.

Reading physical books, on the other hand, provides us with a wide array of benefits. We learn at a youthful age that reading makes us smarter, which is true. Reading:

- *Grows our vocabulary.*

- *Improves comprehension and the ability to follow a conversation or story.*
- *Drastically expands our ability to reason and problem-solve.*
- *Dramatically enhances empathetic reasoning skills.*
- *Increases our cognitive function.*

Reading strengthens pathways that allow for more oxygen to pass through, which can decrease the potential for headaches and migraines while improving our body's overall physicality. For those of us who work out regularly, if we make time to read, too, we'll be more likely to realize the maximum benefit of exercising due to increased and improved connectivity between the brain and the rest of the body.

Reading digital books will provide us with *most* of these benefits, but some of the advantages are lost when we read from a screen as opposed to a page. There is a difference in how our brains process that information, and comprehension may be impacted.[17c]

* * *

BE MINDFUL

Stay aware of how often you're consuming online content, and of how that content makes you feel. Remember the activity you completed in "Fear the Fearmonger," in which you recorded how much time you were dedicating to news consumption, what the sources were, and how you felt? In the early days of decreasing your social media use, consider going through the same process: list the dates and times you used social media, your duration, which platforms you used, and how you felt after interacting on the platform (e.g., tired, calm, content, exhausted, angry, sad). This will help you hold yourself accountable for usage, as well as determine what content or activities are helpful or harmful to your well-being.

* * *

CURATE, CURATE, CURATE

Once you've reflected on how you feel after using social media, take the opportunity to leave behind sources that deplete you. Stop using, delete, or deactivate social accounts that offer you more pain than gain. For the networks you choose to keep, "unlike" or "unfollow" accounts that drain or trigger you, and/or influencers who you feel are too radical, and be increasingly careful about what you share or comment on. However, I will ask that you not "unfriend" or "block" your friends just yet. Remember, you don't want to create a vacuum in which no outside opinions or thoughts can enter. Try, first, to coexist and cooperate.

Know who you're talking to. Is this someone you know "IRL" (in real life)? Is it a bot? Use the "Spot the Bot" app (or similar tools) to become more adept at identifying fake or automated accounts. Those do not count as "friends"—feel free to unfriend and block them.

What about legitimate friends and acquaintances who tend to focus heavily on highly charged political content? Those friends who frequently comment negatively or take part in online arguments? If they pose a danger to your psychological health, you might need to cut them loose. But, if not, I'd urge you not to act too hastily. Think about what you've read so far within these pages. Is there something here that could help you interact with them in a healthy way? Down the line, when you feel ready, they might be the perfect candidate to talk with about ideas and tools within this book. Perhaps you could help them transform in a positive way and end their own civil war?

We need to improve ourselves first. It's like the oxygen mask instructions on an airplane—see to yourself before assisting others. *That's excellent advice.*

Victory:

Play The Only Winning Move

"A strange game.
The only winning move
is not to play."

JOSHUA/WOPR
From the 1983 film "WarGames"

CHAPTER EIGHTEEN

THE ONLY
WINNING MOVE

"Peace is the only battle worth waging."

ALBERT CAMUS

French Author, Journalist, Philosopher

T
he 1983 techno-thriller *WarGames*, written by Lawrence
Lasker and Walter F. Parkes, posed an interesting
question: *Who wins a war?*

In the film, Matthew Broderick plays teenage video game
fanatic and computer hacker David Lightman. While
attempting to gain access to a gaming company's system, to
access as-yet-unreleased games, Lightman stumbles upon an
option titled "Global Thermonuclear War." Intrigued, he runs
the program and takes on the role of the Soviet Union, while the
computer assumes the role of the United States.

What Lightman doesn't realize is that he has unwittingly
hacked a U.S. Military supercomputer, known as the "WOPR"
(War Operation Plan Response), at the North American
Aerospace Defense Command center (NORAD). Not a game at
all, the program he is operating was designed to run simulations

that would assist in predicting, calculating, and waging a nuclear war.

While Lightman is being detained and brought to NORAD, the WOPR continues to run the simulation, calculating potential strikes and counterstrikes, raising the DEFCON (defense readiness condition) alert level as the "war" intensifies.

The film begins with two men in the control room of a nuclear warhead silo, one of whom (played by the late, great John Spencer) refuses to follow an order to turn a key that will launch a nuclear attack. It turns out this directive came as part of a drill, but the defiant act was a malfunction in the system. The glitch? Compassion, self-control, and refusal to participate in an act that could lead to the deaths of "20 million people."

Because of this, changes are made in the system to prevent human interference in the future. So, when NORAD realizes that Lightman's "game" is more than a simulation, and the WOPR is preparing to carry out functions that will launch an actual thermonuclear attack, they are stunned to discover . . . *they have no way to stop it.*

In a last-ditch effort to save humanity, Lightman and the WOPR's original creator attempt to "teach" the computer the futility of war. They do this by asking the WOPR to play itself in a game of tic-tac-toe. The computer quickly cycles through every possible scenario, each time with the same result— "Winner: None."

In the end, the WOPR comes to a prophetic realization: *"The only winning move is not to play."*

The path we're currently on—the civil war we're angling toward—will have no winners. The most important and impactful thing you can do is *not play the game*. Like the man in the film, in the nuclear silo, we must exercise compassion and self-control, and refuse to participate.

It is crucial that we heal the divide, accept one another, recognize that we are a nationwide community, and work toward a time when we can cooperate to achieve mutual goals.

We must stop....

- *Seeing one another as "other"*
- *Constantly fighting in comments sections*
- *Doxing those who support the "wrong" candidate*
- *Refusing to listen to other points of view*
- *Overconsuming information and overusing social media*
- *Slandering the "other side"*

These attitudes and behaviors are only widening the gap. *The only winning move is not to play.* It's time to discontinue behaviors that separate you from other people, no matter how many in your community exhibit them. Someone must wake up first and start doing the right thing: you could be a leader by modeling the right behavior, right now.

Great is the guilt of an unnecessary war.

JOHN ADAMS

MEDITATIONS

ON

PATRIOTISM

"If we love our country, we should also love our countrymen."

RONALD REAGAN

Actor, Union Leader, 40th President of the United States

I t is long past time that we prioritize nation over party. It would be impossible for us to personally know and communicate with every American residing in the United States, but that doesn't mean we can't value each person as a part of our national community, regardless of their political affiliation.

We might not like to think so, but we're all human beings who want the same things: to survive, to thrive, to pursue happiness, and to leave behind a healthy, enduring planet for our children. Political parties have attempted to convince us that we want entirely different things. They focus on what divides us, rather than on what unites us.

> *"[Political parties] are likely in the course of time and things,*
> *to become potent engines, by which cunning, ambitious,*
> *and unprincipled men will be enabled to subvert the power of*
> *the people and to usurp for themselves the reins of government,*
> *destroying afterward the very engines which have*
> *lifted them to unjust dominion."*
> GEORGE WASHINGTON

When we attack other Americans the only people who win are our country's enemies, and we can't solve our nation's problems if we're busy fighting one another. We need to reorient ourselves as a nation, cooperate, and compromise with one another to do what's in the best interest of our entire national community.

Partisanship is the opposite of patriotism. You're either devoted to being a Democrat, Republican, Socialist, Libertarian, OR devoted to being a Patriot—you can't be both.

> **"**
>
> *Too often are we rooting for the pride of a team rather than the good of the nation.*
>
> CRISS JAMI

We must make a conscious and empathetic shift away from trying *to be* right, and toward trying *to do what is right.* Imagine what good could come of us openly sharing thoughts, views, and ideas—working together, even when we disagree, to do what will best serve our national and global communities. When you place loyalty to your party over loyalty to your country, *you are committing an unpatriotic act.*

* * *

What is Patriotism?

I've found most descriptions of patriotism to be vague, lofty, and not particularly helpful. Here is one such definition: "*Patriotism or national pride is the feeling of love, devotion, and sense of attachment to a homeland and alliance with other citizens who share the same sentiment.*"[19a] This doesn't tell me anything about how to conduct myself daily.

Many Americans believe *patriotism* is about pride alone. Others believe it's about fighting for what they believe in. Some will invoke the phrase, "My country, right or wrong." This phrase is bandied about often, but most people aren't truly aware of what it means. It's truncated from a longer phrase, which is "*My country, right or wrong; if right, to be kept right; and if wrong, to be set right.*" It's a quote from 1872, spoken by an American Senator (Carl Schurz).[19b] When people use only the beginning, it would seem to indicate that we should support our country no matter what awful things it might do. The full quote, of course, implies that we have a responsibility to make sure our country is doing what is right. And what is right, right now, is *healing the divide.*

***Being patriotic is about fighting for what is in the best interest
of your fellow Americans, not what is in your personal or partisan
interest.*** Loving the flag, the national anthem, and our troops
shows your pride and support, but true love of country means
loving *your fellow citizens* enough to willingly sacrifice some of
your interests for the betterment of others.

The United States of America has the greatest GDP, the
largest military, is the dominant political force in the world, and
has exported its ideals for one reason and one reason only: *we
cooperate better than anyone else.* "Cooperation" is to incur a cost
for the benefit of someone or something else—and usually
without expectation of anything in return. Within the master
concept of cooperation are thousands of different values which
help to create distinctions and nuances, such as valor, duty,
integrity, diligence, selflessness, kindness, and yes—*patriotism.*

Patriotism is to incur a cost for the benefit of other
Americans. These costs can be tangible, intangible, large, or
minimal. For example:

- *Every time you spend extra time or effort to throw your trash
  in a designated container, rather than on the ground, you're
  incurring a cost.*
- *Every time you give up your time to wait at a stop light,
  rather than speed through it, you're incurring a cost.*
- *Every time you volunteer your time to help those in need,
  rather than stay home and enjoy your day, you're incurring a
  cost.*
- *Every time you pay your taxes, which takes money out of your
  and your family's pockets, you're incurring a cost.*
- *Every time you tell a hard truth, at the expense of your
  reputation, you're incurring a cost.*

Folks like soldiers, teachers, and first responders aren't the only ones who give of themselves. Every day you incur hundreds of micro-costs and make mini sacrifices for the benefit of others. You make conscious decisions that serve the greater good of the country at your own expense. To me, that is patriotism. Each time you perform a patriotic act, you might be unknowingly helping someone else or giving someone else confidence in our structure of cooperation. The only reason our system of governance works is because we all believe that it does—if we cease believing, it will cease to work.

To me, love can be three different things:

1. Decision.
   We make a conscious or unconscious recognition that we love someone or something else.

2. Feeling.
   A powerful emotion increases our inclusive feelings of another.

3. Actions.
   Expending time, money, or energy for the benefit of another, and often without the expectation of anything in return.

I find the decision to love and the feeling of love completely worthless without *commensurate action*. Can you imagine a father telling his kids that he loved them every day while not providing them food, housing, medical care, coaching, advice, education, physical touch, or emotional support? I wish I had more than anecdotal evidence, but most people I have ever heard say "I love my country" also complain most about paying their taxes and express hatred of half our country's citizens.

True love of country is not only about loving the flag, the Statue of Liberty, and first responders, or about supporting the troops and crying during the National Anthem. Patriotism is about sacrificing what might be in your best interest for what is in the best interest of other Americans.

* * *

Vows of a Patriot

True patriotism, to me, is far more than merely flying a flag or professing your love of country. It is showing it in meaningful ways that require a measure of self-sacrifice. It is giving of yourself for the benefit of your fellow citizens.

If we're to do what is right, heal the divide, and watch our country thrive, we must all vow to be truly, *meaningfully* patriotic. **To that end, I humbly offer the following "Vows of a Patriot."**

Notice that these vows are not for your benefit, but the benefit of others. Cooperation works best when everyone is willing to make the same sacrifices. I have taken them, and I encourage others to do the same.

I Vow to Vote

Voting is not only my right but the most powerful instrument of our democracy. I will be informed and always vote, supporting what is in the country's best interest rather than my own.

I Vow to be Inclusive

*Unity is the very price and condition of our survival
and, realizing such, I will support, advance, and
value all Americans.*

I Vow to be Non-Violent

*Violence creates a vicious cycle of vengeance that's
hard to end. Protest is an American value, but protest
should always be peaceful. Violence may only be deployed
as a means of defense, and only as a last resort.*

I Vow to Empathize

*Before I criticize fellow Americans, I will seek first
to understand their experience. Especially in
moments of anxiety and strain, I will strive to be
kind, generous, and considerate.*

I Vow to Compromise

*I recognize that compromise is the price
of cooperation. I will yield my own interests
as necessary for the greater good.*

I Vow to be Truthful

*Deceit is the ultimate threat to our union.
I will actively curate what I believe based on facts
and never deceive another for my own benefit.*

I Vow to Contribute My Share

*I might never fully agree with how our government
spends money, but taxes sustain the institutions and
infrastructure of our democracy. I will pay my share and
advance my grievances to my representative.*

I Vow Never to Disparage
It's my right to criticize ideas, policies, and actions,
but I will not mock, attack, demonize, smear, ridicule,
or vilify another American. I will fight for my ideas,
but I will not fall victim to hate.

I Vow to Put Children First
Every child should have childcare, education, healthcare,
nutrition, and access to developmental activities.

I Vow to do My Duty
No matter what my role, whether parent, teacher,
first responder, worker, student, or citizen,
I will fulfill my obligations, keep my oaths, and never
impede another's ability to do the same.

I Vow to take Responsibility
As a human, I'm bound to make mistakes, but I will
own my blunders, apologize, and make restitutions.
I will not obscure, repudiate, or deflect.

The central notion of patriotism
is not pride, but vowing to contribute
without expectation of return.

CHAPTER TWENTY

WE ARE AMERICANS, DAMMIT

*"A man's country is not a certain area
of land, of mountains, rivers, and woods,
but it is a principle; and patriotism
is loyalty to that principle."*

GEORGE WILLIAM CURTIS
American Writer

S ocially, our views are dependent on the views of those
around us. While I do not think agreeing with everyone in
your neighborhood is of vital importance, I do think it is
valuable for you to surround yourself with people who **believe in
the reunification of the United States** in the same way that you
do. To truly be a successful, unified nation, we need to surround
ourselves with people of a similar goal and remember what we

are thankful for. This will define our social and psychological environment.

I tasked my team with writing up a list of what Americans should be thankful for. Here's what they handed back to me:

Bagels, Baseball, Barbecue, Betty White, Bob Hope, Broadway, Chicken and Waffles, Coffee (to go), Diversity, Dolly Parton, The East Coast, Elvis Presley, Farming, The First Amendment, Freedom, Generosity, The Great Lakes, Hollywood, Hot Dogs, Inclusion, Jazz Music, Louis Armstrong, Lucille Ball, Mark Twain, MLK Jr., The Muppets, Museums, NASA, National Parks, Native Americans, Opportunity, Pie, Prince, Public Libraries, Religious Freedom, Road Trips, Shark Week, The Smithsonian, Southern Hospitality, Stevie Wonder, Summer Vacation, The Star-Spangled Banner, Teddy Bears, Tennessee Williams, Tex-Mex, Thanksgiving, Tom Hanks, The West Coast, Walt Disney.

I looked at that list and one thing stood out to me more than anything else . . . there's nothing here that's partisan. Nothing divisive. These are things we can all agree on, and *that gives me hope.*

America is worth fighting for. If we want to survive, we must come together and stop attacking one another. We must end the divisive partisan conflict, and that starts with each of us— individually.

There's no point in sugar-coating this: not every step of the journey to end your personal civil war will be easy. You might be deeply addicted to news or social media, or feel frequently inclined to both read and participate in the comments sections. You might have negative memories of a person from another political party, causing you to view that affiliation as inherently negative. You will have to do real (often difficult) work, but the end will be well worth the means.

As a brief exercise, I ask that you....

1. Make a list of everything you appreciate about the United States and everything you're thankful for. Make the list as long, short, sentimental, silly, or intellectual as you like, but take the actual activity seriously. *Please complete your list before reading on.*

2. Now that you've completed your list, I will share a few items from my own: the fact that we are a free country (free speech, religion, dress code, etc.); our wide range of terrain and National Parks; our extensive shopping opportunities; cuisine and fast-food chains; diversity; infrastructure; small businesses; cities; opportunities; and sheer abundance.

With your help and involvement in this movement toward reunification, we can end an individualized civil war. All of the qualities we believe make the United States amazing will still exist and will thrive.

* * *

What's Great About America

Thirty-two years ago, I was a plebe Sophomore sitting in the back of a fraternity meeting, consistent with my rank, while the upperclassmen caucused at the front. The meeting was going sideways. We had collectively fallen into a negative bias complaint death spiral. With each comment, everyone hung their heads a little lower.

One of our moral leaders entered the meeting. He quickly assessed what was going on, grabbed the floor, and changed the tenor by listing all the reasons why we were "great." He pointed around the room, sharing inspirational stories about all the wonderful things everyone had done. He transformed the meeting into a celebration. I sat in quiet awe. I will never forget what an inspirational leader he is, and that memory still inspires me today. America is great, in part, because there are amazing leaders like *Eric Rans* for us to emulate.

I don't remember another single minute of the thousands that I spent in fraternity meetings, but that event left an important impression on me. In fact, in a way, it inspired me to write this book. Currently, America is stuck in a "complaint death spiral," but it's never too late for someone to come into the room and say, "Wait a minute? This is who we really are. This is why we're great."

So that's just what I did. I posed the question, on Facebook, to my friends. I asked, "What's great about America?" Here are a few of my favorite responses from that thread:

- *"We are free: speech, religion, to rise above birth circumstances, to travel.... We have incredible abundance in America." - Tom*

- *"Immigrants, we get the job done." - from Hamilton.*

- *"I think one of the best things about America is the diversity. If you are lucky enough to live/work/play in a diverse community, you will see how fascinating it is to open your hearts and minds to cultures, traditions, foods, etc. different than the one you grew up with.... I think The US is one of the only countries that is completely made up of people from many different Nations and Creeds. It's so wonderful to be able to experience and appreciate." - Rocio*

- *"I love that 100 years ago America had enough forethought to create our National Parks system. We now have millions of acres of the most beautiful scenery, wildlife refuges, and spiritual healing places for perpetuity. We need healing places, especially now. Some of the most memorable moments of my life were spent in a National Park." - Mallory*

- *"Here in America, if you dream it you can become it! America is the land of opportunity for those willing to work hard for it!" - Jennifer*

- *"America is still the most resilient modern democracy. They had a revolution against monarchy before almost any other modern republic did, and unlike the French, they had a workable plan to govern out the gate. It took more than a century after that revolution for most European nations to dissolve their monarchies.... America's system of governance has widely discussed flaws, like the electoral college, but it has survived a civil war, two world wars, and a recent insurrection attempt.... I want America to keep succeeding." - Stephen*

- *"This may not be what you're asking, but I regularly feel so lucky to live in a place where I can dress as I like & go where I want, with minimal restrictions. In some countries, what you do, say, wear, and your opportunities as a woman are decided for you.[...] This country certainly isn't perfect and* may fall below some others that have it better, but we've got it pretty good in many ways. There's a long way to go in areas like social justice, but we at least have a system that allows us to better it if we can." - Debbie

- "The US has a positive vibe. Hopeful, can-do and the people, in general, are quite nice." - Marie

- "Wendy's hamburgers with a frosty. Seriously. But, the current political climate is as bad as the coffee Keurig machine in a two-star hotel. Here's to better years ahead." - Paula

- "I say what is great about America is we have the freedom, for now . . . to make a statement that is part wrong and part right. High School Sports, Baseball, Ranches, Our Amazing Cities, Technology, Small Businesses: ALL have greatness AND bad things.... Good and Bad Politicians. And we all have the right to debate these things . . . that is great." - Tim

- "Americans tend to be very optimistic. That optimism helps with the hope for a better tomorrow." - Sergio

It's in that spirit of optimism that I decided to create this guidebook. I do believe we can heal the divide in this country by focusing on what makes it worth the effort.

CHAPTER TWENTY-ONE

FIGHT LIKE CAPTAIN AMERICA

"Heroism is a matter of choice."

RICHARD COHEN

American Journalist

I t is unbelievably important at this specific moment in history to know precisely how to *"fight for what we believe in"* in a productive and unified way. We could all afford to be a little more like a superhero—especially one who wore our nation's colors and followed a moral code that we could all appreciate.

I am, of course, referring to *Marvel's* Captain America, whose values included courage, humility, righteous indignation, sacrifice, and perseverance. Cartoonists Joe Simon and Jack Kirby were on to something when they developed this character—he fights for *all* Americans, not a party, and he has enduring faith in his fellow man. In a recent film adaptation, he psychologically moved to a place beyond war and achieved peace, which is ultimately what we want for all people.

In his book, *The Virtues of Captain America: Modern-Day Lessons on Character from a World War II Superhero*, Mark D. White argues that there can be no better model of ethical behavior today than this character: "Cap's 'old-fashioned' moral code is exactly what we need to restore civility and respect in the 21st century in both our personal lives and our political debates. He is what ancient philosophers—yes, more ancient than Cap—called a moral exemplar." White went on to describe Captain America as "loyal to timeless principles of freedom, equality, and justice." However, he views the character as more than a caricature of over-written patriotism and stressed that he "embodies an inclusive patriotism that balances idealism with clear-eyed pragmatism." [21a]

I want this book to empower you, and the steps within it to bring you peace, so you can empower someone you care about with the knowledge you've received. Much like Captain America's passing of his shield to the "next" Captain America, my great hope is that the ideas contained in this book will be passed on—spread far and wide, to all Americans, so we have a shared tool for helping us reach our ultimate reunification. The undividable **United** States of America.

* * *

How to Fight Like a Superhero

Being a true patriot and modeling patriotic behavior doesn't mean that you can't fight for what you believe in. Even if you've (wisely) decided to abandon partisanship, you don't have to abandon the fight to instill the ideals, policies, and laws you believe will best serve the country and its citizens. The key is to fight effectively. Here's how....

- **DON'T** *argue with friends and family.*
  You won't get far, and we've already covered why this is likely only to further division and kill relationships.

- **DON'T** *create propaganda to help your side "win."*
  It's easy to fall into the trap of thinking, "well, as long as I have good intentions, it's okay." It is not okay. Don't become part of the problem.

- **DON'T** *be a keyboard warrior.*
  Posting on social media relentlessly, refuting posts, commenting, replying, etc. is slacktivism and nothing more. It might give you a false sense that you're *doing something*, but it is wholly ineffectual.

- **DON'T** *protest violently or damage property.*
  The second you participate in acts of violence, vandalism, or destruction, you lose all moral standing and provide fuel for your opposition.

- **DON'T** *counter-protest.*
  There was a time when counter-protesting made sense. Unfortunately, it no longer does. First and foremost, as I mentioned before, the best way to let bad ideas die is to stop giving them attention. I understand how your *cheater detection mechanism* can kick in, creating feelings like *"we've gotta' fight back"* or *"if we don't resist, they'll win"*; however, I strongly suggest that you weigh the following:

What do you have to gain?

- Will you outnumber them and
  shout them down?
  Not likely.

- Will you intimidate them and make them
  think twice before coming out again?
  Even less likely.

- Will you yell better chants than them,
  making them realize the error of their ways
  and change their minds?
  Dream on.

What do you have to lose?

- More attention and division.
  *Nearly guaranteed. Local or national news could
  show up, inviting the issue to be taken up by more
  people. Your counterprotest validates the other
  cause more than empowering your own.*

- Violence.
  *Highly likely. Someone might get hurt—or worse,
  killed—thus inciting the cycle of revenge.*

- A negative perception of your cause.
  *Highly likely. In the heat of the "battle," supporters
  might misbehave, damaging property, harming
  others, or getting arrested. Whoever commits
  violence loses all moral standing.*

Effective fighting techniques are as boring as they are useful
and operative....

- **DO** *attend peaceful rallies and protests.*

  Our right to gather and protest is important, and this can be an effective path to change. But be safe. Commit to protesting peaceably and remove yourself if a counter-protest erupts or the situation becomes dangerous.

- **DO** *obey the law.*

  If law enforcement arrives at your protest or rally, obey all their commands, and *do not ever resist arrest or attack the police.* You are guaranteed to lose. 1,000,000,000% guaranteed.

- **DO** *call your representatives.*

  This is more effective than you realize. Be one of the voices of their constituents that stands out in their mind.

- **DO** *write opinion articles.*

  I don't mean blog posts or social media rants. Research your points, get your proverbial ducks in a row, and create meaningful articles to support your cause. Seek out credible, wide-circulation news sources that will publish your opinion piece.

- **DO** *volunteer.*

  Whether to travel door-to-door or for phone banks. If you want to impact real change, put in the time.

- **DO** *vote.*

  Be an educated, avid voter. This is the cornerstone of democracy, your right, and your responsibility.

CHAPTER TWENTY-TWO

YOU ARE PART OF THE ~~PROBLEM~~ SOLUTION

"It is easy to dodge our responsibilities, but we cannot dodge the consequences of dodging our responsibilities."

SIR JOSIAH STAMP

English Writer, Civil Servant, Statistician, Economist

A s you read this book, you might have experienced a few "ah-ha" or "lightbulb" moments, and even a bit of dread or anxiety at the prospect of discontinuing harmful behaviors or curbing a digital addiction. But if you're still— somewhere in the back of your mind—thinking this country's problems lie on the backs of others, *you really need to think again.*

We. Are. All. Part. Of. The. Problem.

That's ^ not melodrama or hyperbole, it's the unvarnished truth. And while you might not be sitting behind a keyboard purposefully trying to spread misinformation, or storming state buildings, or inciting violence, that does not mean you bear no responsibility for the current state of division in this country. In fact, the inability to see our individual responsibility is, in my estimation, one of our nation's greatest difficulties.

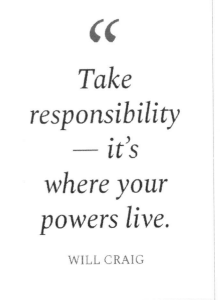

> **"**
>
> *Take responsibility — it's where your powers live.*
>
> WILL CRAIG

There are several key behaviors that I believe contribute most heavily to our country's divide (and brewing civil war). I urge you to read them with an open mind and consider honestly which you might be falling victim to. Then, I urge you to earnestly endeavor to move beyond these behaviors.

HAZARDOUS BEHAVIOR:
Watching five hours of cable news daily.

If you think this is somehow helping, it's not. Frequent consumption of the news and social media only increases our anxiety and fear while decreasing our ability to empathize. In this state, when we finally turn off the television, how can we possibly engage in calm, constructive, meaningful conversation with those who hold alternate views?

How to fix it: Reevaluate how much time you're consuming news, what platforms you're using, and how you're impacting others. Retrain your mind to focus on personal growth, and devote your time elsewhere. *If you're struggling with this, continue to track your consumption and feelings on paper for a while.*

HAZARDOUS BEHAVIOR:
Sitting in your car listening to fearmongering radio.

Again, over-consumption of news is harmful to our psyche, our bodies, and our relationships. Listening to sources rooted in fearmongering or conspiracy is extremely harmful.

How to fix it: Be very honest with yourself about all the different ways you're consuming news: radio, television, social media, from friends, etc. Choose one method to continue using, *minimally,* and spend the rest of your time on other things. Music stimulates our brain in positive ways, stimulating our brain's pleasure and reward centers, so why not spend your commute enjoying your favorite albums?

HAZARDOUS BEHAVIOR:
Talking incessantly about politics and what you saw on the news, reaching out to friends only to complain.

By allowing politics to spill over into other areas of our lives, we can damage relationships and spread anxiety and fear. Though certainly we may have reason, from time to time, to discuss the political climate with our loved ones, excessive and relentless political discourse is as useless as it is annoying.

How to fix it: Think about your relationships over the last six months. What did they look like? What did you do together? What did you talk about? If news and politics featured heavily, it's time to reprioritize and make a concerted effort to alter your behavior. For some, who have descended into almost exclusively discussing the news, this can be a real challenge. While it might sound trivial, consider making a list of topics and questions before heading into conversations. Keep them handy (at least figuratively) so when talk turns to politics you have something to pivot to.

HAZARDOUS BEHAVIOR:
Demonizing the "other" party or viewing them as over-simplified caricatures.

Like late-night television, we find catharsis and confirmation in political cartoons and memes. Though seeing one of these from time to time might be fine, regular observation and sharing of these is harmful, encourages a habit of ridicule, and teaches us to dehumanize others. We begin to see them not as the real, complex, nuanced individuals they are, but instead as over-simplified caricatures based on stereotypes and extremes.

Defeating racism, tribalism, intolerance and all forms of discrimination will liberate us all, victim and perpetrator alike.

BAN KI-MOON

How to fix it: Start becoming aware of just how often you're exposed to this sort of harmful content. If you can identify where/how you're seeing it most often, consider how you might distance yourself from those sources. Pay attention to conversations, as well—are you hearing, sharing, or in any way furthering these distorted views of "others"? Try to discontinue that behavior and adopt the mantra "it stops here." Also, read books that inspire empathy and that will provide you with a less distorted view of others.

HAZARDOUS BEHAVIOR:
Putting the interests of your party above
what is in the best interest of your country.

You might passionately feel that your party's policies and ideals are what's best for the country, and that's okay. What's not okay is putting party before people. Fighting for what you believe in should not include fighting *against others*. The party divide is crushing America, and we're all complicit. Too many are focused on what their party wants—or worse, what the "other" party doesn't want—rather than on what the country needs.

How to fix it: If you truly want this country to succeed, you will need to refocus your mind to seek out and promote what is in the best interest of fellow *citizens* rather than fellow party members. And yes, *sometimes this means promoting ideas or policies that might not directly benefit you.* As the COVID-19 vaccine distribution began, it became clear that my age and health would place me among the last groups to receive it. That was frustrating, but at the same time—I was enormously happy to know that efforts were being made to distribute the vaccine equitably and fairly, even though it would not offer me any advantage. That is the mindset we need to aim for.

HAZARDOUS BEHAVIOR:
Visualizing violence.

This is obvious. If you're envisioning violence, against another political party or otherwise, that's not good. Violence should only be used as a means of defense, and only as a last resort. If you derive pleasure from imagining killing, harming, or eliminating others, that is a very big problem.

How to fix it: First and foremost, I am going to suggest that if this is more than a passing visualization for you, seek out professional help—especially if you envision yourself committing a violent act. If your visualizations are less personal and explicit—and more motivated by a need to "fix" what is broken—that's still not great, but you might be able to work through it on your own. Many otherwise non-violent people have imagined violent ends in recent years, not out of a desire for carnage but out of fear, anxiety, and a genuine desire to fast-forward to a time without conflict. If this sounds like it describes you, think about a time when you were in a terrible argument with someone you loved. How did you work through it? Did you take a break from talking? Did you have a difficult but constructive conversation? Think about what worked for you and consider how you could adapt those behaviors.

HAZARDOUS BEHAVIOR:
Refusing to befriend, or not being able to see value in, those on the "other side."

If you can't see the value in those who think differently than you—if you purposefully avoid striking up relationships with those on the "other" side, or if you've deleted, unfriended, or in some other way disassociated with former friends due to their political allegiances, that's a problem. (For clarity, distancing yourself from a toxic relationship with someone who affiliates with the "other" party is different from cutting off a friendship *simply because* of that affiliation.) But if you're making decisions about who you will associate with based purely on political party, that's dangerous. It demonstrates just how divided our nation has become when we refuse to acknowledge someone's humanity or see them as a whole person, putting party above anything else.

How to fix it: Politics are not everything, and you need to ruminate on that notion. Consider all the other things you might have in common with someone, from shared hobbies to backgrounds, philosophies, or aspirations. Not all differences portend an "impossible" relationship, and what a boring world it would be if they did! We grow through exposure to more people, more ideas, and more experiences. Keep reading books and watching stories (movies, documentaries, or television shows) about people and characters who are different than you in some way. If you feel yourself judging them, stop and ask yourself *why*. Your mindset, acceptance, inclusivity, and empathy will change positively over time. *Everyone brings value, no matter what their political affiliation might be.* A house isn't built by one person—it takes designers, architects, engineers, craftsman, carpenters, plumbers . . . the list goes on and on. It's the same for our country. Where we are great, we are great because of our rich differences, not despite of them.

HAZARDOUS BEHAVIOR:
Taking pleasure in the failure of others or the "other" party.

If you've ever laughed at or found enjoyment in the "other" party failing, that's a problem. There is an enormous difference between feeling relief that a policy you were concerned about did not come to pass and deriving *pleasure* from the failure of those who promoted it. "Thank goodness that law didn't pass" is vastly different from "Ha-ha! The other party didn't get their way!" If you often experience the second reaction, your priorities may be askew.

How to fix it: For some, this won't be an easy fix. You're going to need to take a long, hard look at what motivates you, where you might be prioritizing "winning" over what's right, and how you can better understand and empathize with others. A good starting point is reading—books on empathy, or books to help you understand the plight of those you must admit you don't (yet) care for or about. Consider finding ways to personally interact with those you consider "other." Anything you can do to increase your understanding and empathy is extremely important work that will benefit you, your community, and your country.

HAZARDOUS BEHAVIOR:
Deriving enjoyment from ridiculing others.

Deliberately mocking, shaming, and shunning others is how our social divide was created in the first place. We might not always agree with someone, but we should not want them to suffer. If ridiculing others excites you, it's important to figure out why that is.

How to fix it: Start by asking yourself *why*. Why are you behaving this way? What about it excites you? What are you feeling while you ridicule someone? How are you ridiculing them? How are they reacting? What provoked your behavior in the first place? The answers to these questions could be very revealing and indicate an underlying need, fear, or concern.

HAZARDOUS BEHAVIOR:
Calling others "sheeple."

We have all been indoctrinated in some way, and anyone can fall victim to propaganda. Showing empathy to those who are experiencing it is the only way to help them, not by shaming. Also, I hate to be the bearer of bad news, but often the person hurling this insult is just as underinformed, misinformed, or in some way *"towing the party line."*

How to fix it: Just *stop*. Refer back to the section above on ridiculing. Going forward, whenever you have the urge to resort to this insult, stop and ask yourself, *"Is this person genuinely falling victim to herd mentality, or am I just unhappy with their position?"* If the former, ask yourself, *"Will insulting them in this way help anything?"* Spoiler alert: The answer is *NO*.

HAZARDOUS BEHAVIOR:
Pointing the finger and blaming "them"
for all our country's troubles.

Blame is unproductive. You really have no right to complain about this country's problems if you're not actively working to fix them, and you can't do that if you feel you bear no responsibility. As Deepak Chopra said, *"When you blame and criticize others, you are avoiding some truth about yourself."*[22a] There are always areas for improvement in your own life, ways in which you've caused harm, or areas where you have fallen short.

How to fix it: Take steps to dig yourself out of the stagnant cesspool of blame. It's easy to stand back and point the finger; it's much harder to take responsibility for improving things—but it's the only thing that is going to work. Determining who bears the most accountability for getting us here is useless; what's important is doing the individual work to get us out. Take the steps in this book first, and, once you've reached a place where you feel *your* civil war has ended, you can model more patriotic behaviors for others, and share your journey in the hope that they, too, can heal.

HAZARDOUS BEHAVIOR:
You feel the need to exact revenge in the name of "justice."

Revenge is about retaliation; *justice* is about restoring balance. Knowing the difference is key. There have been injustices committed in our country by citizens, businesses, and politicians, and you might feel that "payback" is right and just. But while we have a rule of law, no person or institution is above that law, and anyone who has broken it must be held to account: that is not the same as *vengeance*, nor is it your responsibility to carry it out. Justice must be served in the correct way, via rational, objective, non-partisan institutions.

How to fix it: Try to resist the urge for revenge and understand that in seeking it you harm yourself. Studies have shown that those who are successful in exacting revenge do not feel better, but *worse*. Recognize that if justice is to be served, it should be done through the proper channels and do not attack the process.[22b]

HAZARDOUS BEHAVIOR:
Tying your identity to a party label.

When I see people waving flags, wearing clothing, and painting their faces with party slogans, it reminds me of fans at a sporting event. Surely you, like me, know at least one person whose identity is so interwoven with their team pride that even their home is decorated with mascots and team colors. When did this happen? How did American politics get here? Once we've committed to a party in such a passionate, "devoted, right or wrong" sort of way—once it becomes tribal—we begin to lose the ability to think clearly and for ourselves. It's also dangerously easy to develop "tunnel vision," in which we only view news that interests our political party, or read news that favors our party, or follow and associate with those who also identify with our party. When we're only concerned with "our team," we leave half the country to flounder.

How to fix it: Start by realizing that you are a nuanced, complicated, interesting human being—*that* is your identity, not your party, (nor the colors of your favorite sports team). Start genuinely studying what your party stands for, and the policies and politicians it is promoting. Make sure that your support is based on your thoughtful agreement that those policies and politicians are genuinely in the best interest of the nation. Perhaps you will find that it *is*, and that's fabulous. But many get so caught up in the "sport" of party support that they forget why they began supporting that party in the first place. I will also suggest that you look carefully and thoughtfully, with an open mind, at the policies and politicians of "other" parties. Try to do so without the lens of trying to find fault. You could come away feeling exactly as you did before, or you might find that you genuinely see value in some ideas floated by the "other" side. If so, remember that affiliating with a party doesn't mean you must vote directly down party lines. If you're truly invested in the best interest of our nation, you should be willing to at least *entertain* the notion of non-partisan voting. By working together as people, rather than parties, we can get much more done, more effectively.

HAZARDOUS BEHAVIOR:
Believing this country can't go on with, or that you can't continue to live here with, "them."

Feeling hopeless, cynical, and closed-off are all signs of a lack of social empathy. You may have lost faith in others to help improve the situation, and when you consider making a change in your own life, you question "*what difference will it make?*"

How to fix it: Think seriously about what you love about this country, and what is at stake. Remind yourself that on the other end of the spectrum there's someone in the "other" camp feeling the same way that you are—and they are not the over-simplified, extremist caricature some would make them out to be. They're

America was not built on fear. America was built on courage, on imagination and an unbeatable determination to do the job at hand.

HARRY S. TRUMAN

just like *you*. They want this country to succeed, too; they just have different ideas about what route will get us there. If that's true, surely there is common ground to be found, surely, you're not all *that* different, and surely you want the same things in a larger sense. For me, knowing that there are others who feel just as convicted about fighting for what I feel passionate about dismantling gives me a strange sense of hope. It helps me realize that I must view things through a different lens, both in terms of where I might be wrong and where "they" might be right.

Imagine what could be accomplished if we all made the effort—**there is hope, and it starts with *you*.**

CHAPTER TWENTY-THREE

#Undividable

"A house divided against itself cannot stand."

ABRAHAM LINCOLN

16*th* *President of the United States of America*

O ne of my favorite quotes comes from the film *The American President*, written by the incomparable Aaron Sorkin. In an impassioned speech, President Andrew Shepherd (played brilliantly by Michael Douglas) claims, "America isn't easy. America is advanced citizenship. You've got to want it bad because it's gonna put up a fight. It's gonna say, *You want free speech? Let's see you acknowledge a man whose words make your blood boil who is standing center stage and advocating at the top of his lungs that which you would spend a lifetime opposing at the top of yours.*"

I love that term—"advanced citizenship." And I fully agree, America is many things—*the melting pot, country of opportunity, land of the free, home of the brave*—but "easy" isn't one of them. That's because we're not a dictatorship or a monarchy, we are a democracy, and that means *each and every one of* us has a responsibility to ensure its survival.

While I'm not a fan of broad generalizations or stereotyping, I think we can agree that, throughout the world, citizens of certain countries are "known for" certain things. For example....

- GERMANY: *Precision*
- CANADA: *Friendliness*
- BRAZIL: *Fun*
- SWITZERLAND: *Neutrality*
- BRITAIN: *Tradition*
- JAPAN *Deference*
- UNITED STATES: *Optimism*

Optimism is our ***national superpower.*** No matter how bad it was yesterday, we believe that we can wake up, dust ourselves off, and make tomorrow better than today. Setbacks are temporary, failures build character, the path of least resistance is for the weak, and defeat is temporary.

Allow me to flaunt my *American optimism* for a moment. We are equal to the task of "advanced citizenship." I believe in this nation, and I believe in its citizens. There is more that unites us than divides us. I believe that Democrats, Republicans, and Independents all want the same things, and I believe that we can find common ground.

Our war is not with one another, and anyone who would sell you that notion is not worthy of your time, money, or attention.

We must abandon our current perspective—Democrats seeing one country, Republicans seeing an entirely different country, and both thinking the other is taking it to hell in a handbasket. *It just isn't so.* This mindset is a result of an increasingly obstructed view, deliberately painted for us by fearmongers. We must clear our vision. It's time to wake up, blink, and begin to see more clearly that there is one America, that we are not grotesque stereotypes, and that there *is* common ground.

We are Americans, and we must stand united against those who would seek to divide us. We must embrace the truth that there is one *undividable* America, and we must *live that truth* relentlessly. Let it be our rallying cry! It's time to reclaim our power, work together, and proceed—undividable.

I am optimistic.
I believe that we can.

LEARN MORE AT

www.SecondCivilWar.co

SOURCES

1a - Rasmussen Reports - 2018 (https://tinyurl.com/43bybw58)

1b - Northwestern - "Study: Republicans and Democrats hate the other side more than they love their own side" - Stephanie Kulke - 2020 (https://tinyurl.com/yrs453c9)

1c - Pew Research - Partisanship and Political Animosity in 2016 (https://tinyurl.com/46pkpebx)

1d - The Perception Gap - "More in Common" poll - 2019 (https://tinyurl.com/4mth8aya)

1e - Pew Research - Gun Policy Remains Divisive, But Several Proposals Still Draw Bipartisan Support - 2018 (https://tinyurl.com/3rmenpju)

1f - Pew Research - Majorities See Government Efforts to Protect the Environment as Insufficient - 2018 (https://tinyurl.com/3u7sknzk)

1g - Pew Research - Two-Thirds of Americans Think Government Should Do More on Climate - 2020 (https://tinyurl.com/ukzvr4ut)

1h - Pew Research - Americans agree on trade: Good for the country, but not great for jobs - 2014 (https://tinyurl.com/49s8ftef)

1i - Pew Research - Most Say Immigration Policy Needs Big Changes - 2013 (https://tinyurl.com/peujj4e8)

1j - Pew Research - How Americans see problems of trust - 2019 (https://tinyurl.com/84a5a4fe)

1k - Harvard Kennedy School - Reimagining Rights and Responsibilities in the United States - 2020 (https://tinyurl.com/x6pszp9h)

1l - Gallup – "Party Groups Agree on Importance of Big Election Issues" - Lydia Saad - 2016 (https://tinyurl.com/53x27kvm)

1m - University of Maryland School of Public Policy - Americans on Nuclear Weapons - 2020 (https://tinyurl.com/ymubwu7a)

1n - University of Maryland School of Public Policy - Americans agree on police reforms that have divided Washington, new poll shows - 2020 (https://tinyurl.com/56wdrska)

1o - Pew Research – "Far more Americans see 'very strong' partisan conflicts now than in the last two presidential election years" - Katherine Schaeffer - 2020 (https://tinyurl.com/2tvu6bs4)

2a - Sapiens - "Cultivating Peace in the Heart of the Balkans" - Jordan Kiper - 2019 (https://tinyurl.com/v6wrwpec)

2b - BBC News - "Rwanda genocide: 100 days of slaughter" - 2019 (https://tinyurl.com/y7wua29z)

2c - National Park Service, U.S. Department of the Interior - "Death and Dying" - Drew Gilpin Faust (https://tinyurl.com/3kr6dt47)

4a - The Guardian – "'I had no qualms': The people turning in loved ones for the Capitol attack" – Kari Paul - 2021 (https://tinyurl.com/46bzbay3)

4b - Los Angeles Daily News – "First mugshot: What 'QAnon shaman' Jacob Chansley looks like out of costume" - Associated Press - 2021 (https://tinyurl.com/yenjppjr)

4c - Politico – "'He has an obligation to them': Attorney for 'QAnon shaman' asks Trump to pardon rioters" - Quint Forgey - 2021 (https://tinyurl.com/uapkvwjj)

4d - Washington Post - "Legally, Pence cannot overturn the election for Trump" - Ann E. Marimow - 2021 (https://tinyurl.com/mjzr3te9)

4e - AP News - "Man who wore horns, hat apologizes for storming Capitol" - Jacques Billeaud - 2021 (https://tinyurl.com/68sdhffd)

4f - Business Insider - "A Capitol riot suspect known as the 'QAnon Shaman' said he was 'deeply disappointed' in Trump for not being 'honorable'" - Lauren Frias -2021 (https://tinyurl.com/dsr5a8j6)

5a - Atomic Habits - James Clear (https://tinyurl.com/4u5m5wff)

5b - New York Times - Are You 'Virtue Signaling'? - Jillian Jordan and David Rand – 2019 (https://tinyurl.com/yp3v8ux7)

5c - Insider – "Politicians and influencers have been accused of 'virtue signaling' during police brutality protests, but the callouts could do more harm than good" - Rachel E. Greenspan - 2020 (https://tinyurl.com/9s7yfb4)

5d - The Guardian - "'Virtue-signalling' - the putdown that has passed its sell-by date" - David Shariatmadari - 2016 (https://tinyurl.com/pws2anxp)

5e - NPR - 'Useful Delusions' Examines How Beliefs Can Be Powerful In Positive And Negative Ways - Steve Inskeep - 2021(https://tinyurl.com/2ucyztp2)

7a - Forbes - "Societies That Promote Openness And Tolerance Are Happier, According To New Research" - Mark Travers - 2020 (https://tinyurl.com/khjhvhd6)

7b - Making Sense - "Can We Pull Back From The Brink?" - Sam Harris - 2020 (https://tinyurl.com/trwx9wy8)

7c - For a more comprehensive list, please visit https://en.wikipedia.org/wiki/United_States_free_speech_exceptions

7d - J. Krishnamurti, Public Talk, December 1933 (https://tinyurl.com/4twkkjcp)

7e - Simply Psychology - Maslow's Hierarchy of Needs - Dr. Saul McLeod - 2020 (https://tinyurl.com/k9pedds5)

7f - Good Reads - The Gifts of Imperfection - Brené Brown (https://tinyurl.com/88dpd4)

8a - Medium - 100 Awesome Freethought Quotes - Hein de Haan - 2019 (https://tinyurl.com/u8rb87t6)

8b - James Clear – "Why Facts Don't Change Our Minds" - James Clear (https://tinyurl.com/z3y2xfkf)

8c - James Clear – "Why Facts Don't Change Our Minds" - James Clear (https://tinyurl.com/z3y2xfkf)

8d - Check out the Cognitive Bias Codex here: https://tinyurl.com/hpta8kvk

8e - The Balance – "How Every President Since Hoover Has Affected the Economy" - Kimberly Amadeo - 2020 (https://tinyurl.com/2vff5m5w)

8f - Our World in Data - Human Rights - Max Roser - 2018 (https://tinyurl.com/rpwtnsct)

8g - The Balance - "Unemployment Rate by Year Since 1929 Compared to Inflation and GDP" - Kimberly Amadeo - 2021 (https://tinyurl.com/yjk6s2zc)

8h - Forbes - "We Looked At How The Stock Market Performed Under Every U.S. President Since Truman – And The Results Will Surprise You" - 2020 (https://tinyurl.com/4kbcmceb)

8i - Barron's - "The Stock Market Doesn't Care Who the President Is" – Ben Levisohn - 2020 (https://tinyurl.com/hrd4ejwx)

8j - Our World in Data - Economic Growth – Max Roser (https://tinyurl.com/4cfbfnf9)

8k - New York Times - "Presidents Have Less Power over the Economy Than You Might Think" - Neil Irwin - 2017 (https://tinyurl.com/5zvrmds4)

8l - Chicago Tribune - "What impact does the president have on the labor market?" - Noah Smith - 2017 (https://tinyurl.com/srueryw9)

9a - PBS Newshour - What is Newsworthy? (https://tinyurl.com/478yd97y)

9b - Refinery29 - "The People Who Created Facebook & YouTube Are Sorry" - Mirel Zaman - 2020 (https://tinyurl.com/wwvtwp9f)

9c - Fortune - "Are you willing to pay for news? The future of journalism may depend on it" - Jennifer Hoewe, Brett Sherrick - 2020 (https://tinyurl.com/kym8xewc)

9d - Developmental Science - "Three-month-olds show a negativity bias in their social evaluations" - J. Kiley Hamlin, Karen Wynn, Paul Bloom - 2010 (https://tinyurl.com/mna9ymve)

9e - USA Today - "How I kicked my news addiction" - Jeff Stibel - 2018 (https://tinyurl.com/t3am6b3m)

9f - UPI - Study: Americans apathetic over world news - 2002 (https://tinyurl.com/yjfy4729)

12a - BBC - "Myanmar coup: How Facebook became the 'digital tea shop'" - Saira Asher - 2021 (https://tinyurl.com/rfx52bnc)

12b - BBC - "Myanmar coup: How Facebook became the 'digital tea shop'" - Saira Asher - 2021 (https://tinyurl.com/rfx52bnc)

12c - New York Times – "Facebook Admits It Was Used to Incite Violence in Myanmar" - Alexandra Stevenson - 2018 (https://tinyurl.com/5h7nb7mv)

12d - New York Times – "Facebook Fueled Anti-Refugee Attacks in Germany, New Research Suggests" - Taub, Fisher - 2018 (https://tinyurl.com/3prz4pus)

13a - Washington Post - "Come On, Howard, Say You're Sorry" - 1983 (https://tinyurl.com/7bhwt4pd)

13b - Washington Post - "Come On, Howard, Say You're Sorry" - 1983 (https://tinyurl.com/7bhwt4pd)

13c - Open Culture - John Cleese's Comedically Explains the Psychological Advantages of Extremism: "It Makes You Feel Good Because It Provides You with Enemies" - 2020 (https://tinyurl.com/4ckdkd73)

13d - Avira - "How to spot a bot on social media" - Diana Plutis - 2020 (https://tinyurl.com/5rkcd78k)

13e - Science – "Sweet Revenge?" - Brian Knutson - 2004 (https://tinyurl.com/4t2ha4c5)

14a - NPR - "More Americans Than You Might Think Believe in Conspiracy Theories" - Shankar Vedantam - 2014 (https://tinyurl.com/7pp3kp9e)

15a - Laird Wilcox - What is "Political Extremism"? - Laird Wilcox (https://tinyurl.com/ba9rntnp)

16a - Mashable - "YouTube will now disable comments on all videos featuring children" - Matt Binder - 2019 (https://tinyurl.com/ynh74wjx)

17a - Chicago Tribune - "Phone noises, notifications are stressing you out—but so is silence" - Sammy Caiola - 2017 (https://tinyurl.com/vpb93uyr)

17b - Statista - 2021 (https://tinyurl.com/4tey62er)

17c - Healthline - "Digital Reading Can Cause You to Miss the Bigger Picture" - Brian Krans - 2016 (https://tinyurl.com/3muvn9nc)

19a - Wikipedia - Patriotism (https://tinyurl.com/9hemfwnm)

19b - Oxford Reference - Patriotism - Carl Schurz - 1872 (https://tinyurl.com/2zhs5brw)

21a - The New Republic - "The Moral Philosophy of Captain America" - John Gray - 2014 (https://tinyurl.com/2h4m383h)

22a - Deepak Chopra - Some Truth About You - Deepak Chopra (https://tinyurl.com/putr6bz)

22b - Washington Post - "Why getting even may make you feel worse in the long run" - Jennifer Berheny Wallace - 2017 (https://tinyurl.com/4y7m5mez)

Contact

Peter Montoya works with organizations, businesses, and teams to develop powerful cooperators who unite people behind common goals. For permission to use Peter's work, or to request an interview, a speaking engagement (live or virtual), or for other requests of a similar nature, please scan: